DECLARER PLAY AT BRIDGE
A QUIZBOOK

BARBARA SEAGRAM • DAVID BIRD

MASTER POINT PRESS • TORONTO, CANADA

Master Point Press
331 Douglas Ave.
Toronto, Ontario, Canada
M5M 1H2   (416)781-0351

Email: info@masterpointpress.com

Websites: www.masterpointpress.com
                 www.teachbridge.com
                 www.bridgeblogging.com
                 www.ebooksbridge.com

Library and Archives Canada Cataloguing in Publication

Seagram, Barbara
        Declarer play at bridge : a quizbook / Barbara Seagram
and David Bird.

Issued also in electronic formats.
ISBN 978-1-897106-91-4

        1. Contract bridge. I. Bird, David, 1946- II. Title.

GV1282.3.S417 2012   795.41'53   C2012-906096-8

We acknowledge the financial support of the Government of Canada through the Book Publishing Industry Development Program (BPIDP) for our publishing activities.

Editor   Ray Lee
Copy editor/interior format   Sally Sparrow
Cover and interior design   Olena S. Sullivan/New Mediatrix

2 3 4 5 6   18 17 16 15 14

PRINTED IN CANADA

CONTENTS

FOREWORD

The problems in most bridge quiz books are difficult. Sometimes they are absurdly difficult and even expert players are forced to shrug their shoulders and turn the page to read the answer. Will that happen to you when you tackle the problems in this particular book? No! The solution to every problem is a relatively straightforward application of techniques such as ruffing losers, taking finesses and discarding losers. In the section on notrump play, you will also need to hold up stoppers and take some finesses into the safe defender's hand. It is very important that you make a plan for every contract. In particular, you will often have to think carefully about the entries that you need to both hands.

Perhaps there will be problems that you do not get right first time. Excellent! You will get them right the second time, also when you next encounter such situations at the table. Improving your game is the purpose of a book like this.

We address all the important basic techniques of play in suit and notrump contracts. Once you have mastered these, you can be sure that your play will be better than that of most of the players you face.

The time has come for you to attempt the first problem. Good luck, remember to make a plan at the start of each contract and… enjoy yourself!

Barbara Seagram and David Bird

PART 1

SUIT CONTRACTS

1

COUNTING LOSERS TO PLAN A SUIT CONTRACT

The best way to plan a suit contract is to start by counting the tricks that you might lose. You look at the hand with the longer holding in the trump suit (usually your own hand, as declarer) and — suit by suit — count the potential losers.

Suppose you are in 4♠ (played by South, as always in a bridge book) and have this diamond suit:

◇ 8 5 2

◇ A 10 6

You would make a note that you start with 'two diamond losers'. The ace will win one round of the suit, but your ◇10 and ◇6 are potential losers on subsequent rounds.

Let's say that this is your heart holding:

♡ K 9 2

♡ A 7 5

You have 'one heart loser'. Although the heart holding in declarer's hand (A75) contains two losers, one of them is covered by dummy's king. You could score the ace and king on the first two rounds but would then have a loser on the third round. Although you look at the losers in your own hand (usually the long-trump declarer's hand), you make allowance for any losers that are covered by honors in the dummy.

Perhaps you also have this club suit:

♣ A K 7

♣ Q 4

You have only two clubs in your hand, so the maximum number of club losers would be two. As it happens, dummy has the ace and king opposite, so you have no losers at all in clubs. Indeed, you have a surplus winner in dummy, which may allow you to discard a loser in some different suit.

Now let's combine those three side-suit holdings. Here are two hands on which you might have bid to 4♠:

♠ J 8 6 4
♡ K 9 2
◇ 8 5 2
♣ A K 7

♠ K Q 10 9 3
♡ A 7 5
◇ A 10 6
♣ Q 4

West	North	East	South
			1♠
pass	3♠	pass	4♠
all pass			

Suppose that West leads the ◇K. Before playing a card from dummy, you should stop to make a plan. The first step is to count the potential losers in the long-trump hand (South on this deal).

You have one loser in spades. You will lose a trick to the ace of trumps but the remainder of the suit will then be yours. As we noted on the previous page, you have one loser in hearts, two possible losers in diamonds and none in clubs. You would mentally note this loser position:

Losers: ♠ 1   ♡ 1   ◇ 2   ♣ 0   Total: 4

You have four potential losers and in a contract of 4♠ you can afford to lose only three tricks. You must therefore make a plan to avoid one of the losers. On this particular deal, your eventual intention would be to discard a heart or diamond loser on dummy's surplus winner in clubs.

How does the play go? You win the diamond lead with the ace and play a trump. You should always draw trumps first unless there is a good reason not to do so. The defenders are welcome to win with the ♠A and to cash two diamond tricks. When you regain the lead, you will draw the outstanding trumps and then play the ♣Q, followed by the ♣A and ♣K. On the third round of clubs you will discard a heart.

Look back at the summary of your possible losers above. You did lose one spade and two diamonds. You managed to avoid a heart loser, by discarding it on the surplus club winner, and therefore restricted your total losers to three. Contract made! This was the plan that you executed:

PLAN: I will draw trumps and discard a loser on the third round of clubs.

The next chapter will contain several quiz hands where you can make the contract by discarding one or more losers. Before you attempt these problems, we will give you some more practice in counting losers.

> ♠ J 9 6 3
> ♡ Q 9 7 4
> ◇ 8 5 2
> ♣ K 7

> ♠ 5
> ♡ A K J 10 8 3
> ◇ A 9 6
> ♣ A 10 4

West leads the ◇Q against your contract of 4♡. Looking at each suit in turn, how many potential losers are there in the South hand? What is the total number of losers? Carry on reading when you have decided on your answers.

In spades, you have only one loser. There could not possibly be more because you have only one spade in your hand; you will be able to ruff the second round of spades. There are no losers in hearts, the trump suit. In diamonds, the ace will win the first round, so you are left with two potential losers. In clubs, the ♣10 and the ♣4 are losers but one of them is covered by dummy's king. You therefore have one loser in clubs. This is the situation:

Losers: ♠ 1   ♡ 0   ◇ 2   ♣ 1   Total: 4

In a later chapter we will make a plan to reduce these four losers to the required three. (In short, you will ruff a club loser in dummy.)

Here is another hand, this time played in a lowly partscore contract:

```
        ♠ A Q 6 3
        ♡ Q 7 6 4
        ◇ 10 5
        ♣ 10 9 5

        ♠ 8 7
        ♡ K 3
        ◇ K Q J 9 6 4 2
        ♣ J 2
```

West leads the ♡J against 3◇. Looking at each suit in turn, how many possible losers do you have?

In spades you have one loser. You have two spades in your hand and one of them is covered by dummy's ♠A. In hearts you have one loser. You expect to lose a trick to the ♡A but you can win the second round with one of your honors. In diamonds you have one loser, to the defenders' ◇A. In clubs there are two potential losers. This is the loser summary:

Losers: ♠ 1   ♡ 1   ◇ 1   ♣ 2   Total: 5

There are five potential losers and in a contract of 3◇ you can afford only four losers. Once again, we will see in a later chapter what plan you should make for this contract. (It will involve taking a finesse in spades — in other words, leading a low spade from your hand and playing dummy's ♠Q, hoping that it will win.)

POINTS TO REMEMBER

- The first step in planning a suit contract is to count your losers.

- You look at the hand with the longer trump holding — usually declarer's hand. You then count how many potential losers there are in each suit.

- If the total number of losers is more than you can afford in your chosen contract, you must make a plan to avoid one or more losers.

- There are three main ways of avoiding a loser. So far we have seen an example of one of these: discarding a loser on a surplus winner. In later chapters we will look at the other two: ruffing (trumping) losers in the dummy and finessing.

2

DISCARDING LOSERS

In this chapter you can test yourself on several contracts where you can succeed by discarding one or more losers. For each problem, you should start by making a plan. This will involve counting your potential losers and then seeing how you can reduce this number to allow you to make the contract.

After forming a general plan, you must decide the order of play. This will usually involve drawing trumps immediately unless there is some good reason not to do so.

PROBLEM 1

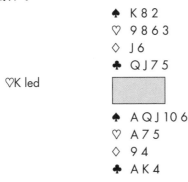

♠ K 8 2
♡ 9 8 6 3
◇ J 6
♣ Q J 7 5

♡K led

♠ A Q J 10 6
♡ A 7 5
◇ 9 4
♣ A K 4

West	North	East	South
			1♠
pass	2♠	pass	4♠
all pass			

Your 1♠ opening bid promises at least five cards in the suit. North has a minimum responding hand with three-card spade support and raises to 2♠. With 18 HCP including plenty of top honors, you are then worth a jump to game in spades.

What is the first thing you should do when West leads the ♡K? Perhaps your answer is: 'I think I'll win with the ♡A.' That's not exactly the answer that we were hoping for. The first thing you should do is, yes, make a plan!

Count the potential losers in each suit to find the total number of losers. If the total is more than three (the number of tricks that you can afford to lose in a major-suit game), you must make a plan to avoid one or more losers.

When you have made a plan for this contract and decided what your order of play will be, you can take a look at the solution on the next page.

SOLUTION 1

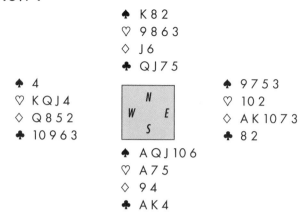

♠ K 8 2
♥ 9 8 6 3
♦ J 6
♣ Q J 7 5

♠ 4
♥ K Q J 4
♦ Q 8 5 2
♣ 10 9 6 3

♠ 9 7 5 3
♥ 10 2
♦ A K 10 7 3
♣ 8 2

♠ A Q J 10 6
♥ A 7 5
♦ 9 4
♣ A K 4

West leads the ♡K against your spade game. Before playing a card from dummy, you must make a plan. In a suit contract, the first step is to count your losers in each suit. You look at the hand with more trumps (usually called the 'long-trump hand'). Most of the time this will be your hand as declarer — the South hand here. You see that you have no spade losers. You have three cards in hearts and the ace is a winner, leaving you with two losers. In diamonds you have two losers; in clubs you have no losers. This is the position:

Losers: ♠0 ♡2 ◇2 ♣0 Total: 4

You have four possible losers and must reduce this to three. Look at the club suit. You have three clubs in your hand with four in the dummy. You have four winners in the suit. This means that on the fourth round of clubs, you will be able to discard one of the losers in the South hand. This will reduce your loser total to the required three.

How does the play go? You win the first trick with the ♡A and draw trumps immediately. This is always the first thing to do unless you can see a good reason not to do so. Suppose you forgot to draw trumps for some reason, and started to play your club winners instead. Disaster! East would trump (or 'ruff', which means the same thing) the third round and the defenders would score four more tricks in the red suits to put you two down.

You win the heart lead with the ace, cross to the ♠K and lead back to the ♠A. When West shows out, you must play two more rounds of trumps to draw all of East's trumps. You continue with the ♣A and the ♣K, (playing the high cards from the hand with fewer cards in the suit, called the 'short side'). The way is then clear for you to cross to the ♣Q and to play the ♣J, throwing a diamond or a heart.

PLAN: I will draw trumps and then play four rounds of clubs, throwing one of my red-suit losers.

PROBLEM 2

```
                  ♠ A 8 2
                  ♡ K 6 4
                  ◇ Q 9 7 2
                  ♣ 8 4 3
♠Q led        ┌─────────────┐
              │             │
              └─────────────┘
                  ♠ 9 4
                  ♡ A Q J 7 5 3
                  ◇ A K
                  ♣ K 7 5
```

West	North	East	South
			1♡
pass	2♡	pass	4♡
all pass			

As on the previous problem, South is strong enough to go to game when partner raises hearts to the two-level. West leads the ♠Q and you pause to make a plan. How many potential losers do you have?

There is one loser in spades and none in hearts. You have no diamond losers but three possible losers in clubs — your king may take a trick but you cannot count on it. This is the situation:

Losers: ♠ 1   ♡ 0   ◇ 0   ♣ 3   Total: 4

What plan should you make? One possible way of saving a club loser would be to lead from the dummy towards the ♣K (a type of finesse). If you were lucky and East held the ♣A, you would score a trick with your king and lose only two tricks in the suit. No one likes to rely on luck when there is a better chance available. Can you see one?

You have only two diamonds in your hand and a total of three top diamond winners. In other words, you have a surplus diamond winner (the ◇Q) on which you may be able to discard one of your black-suit losers. Can you see a plan that would allow you to score three diamond tricks?

SOLUTION 2

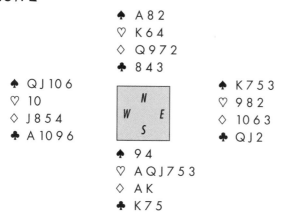

```
              ♠ A 8 2
              ♡ K 6 4
              ◇ Q 9 7 2
              ♣ 8 4 3
♠ Q J 10 6                    ♠ K 7 5 3
♡ 10          N              ♡ 9 8 2
◇ J 8 5 4   W   E            ◇ 10 6 3
♣ A 10 9 6      S            ♣ Q J 2
              ♠ 9 4
              ♡ A Q J 7 5 3
              ◇ A K
              ♣ K 7 5
```

West leads the ♠Q against your heart game and this is the loser position:

Losers: ♠ 1   ♡ 0   ◇ 0   ♣ 3   Total: 4

Leading towards the ♣K in the hope of avoiding a club loser will rely on luck. When the cards lie as in the diagram, West will win with the ♣A and you will go down. A better idea is to discard a black-suit loser on dummy's surplus diamond winner. How should the play go?

Suppose you win the spade lead and draw trumps in three rounds. You will not be able to score three diamond tricks. After playing the ◇A and ◇K, you would have no entry to dummy to reach the ◇Q. You need to find a way of crossing to dummy after you have played the two diamond winners in your hand.

You must use the ♡K as an entry to the ◇Q. After winning the spade lead, you draw two rounds of trumps with the ace and queen (retaining dummy's king as an entry for later). Even though the trumps break 3-1 and there is still a trump out, you must then play the ◇A and ◇K.

Next you cross to dummy with the ♡K, drawing the last trump. You then play the ◇Q and discard a spade (or a club). With ten tricks assured, you can lead towards the ♣K to seek an overtrick. The king loses to the ace, but this is good news in a way. It means that your play of using the ♡K as an entry to take a discard was the only way to make the contract.

> **PLAN: I will win the spade lead and play the ace and queen of trumps. After playing the ◇A and ◇K, I will cross to the king of trumps to discard a loser on the ◇Q.**

POINT TO REMEMBER

When a side suit is blocked and you need to use a trump as a dummy entry, you may not be able to draw all the trumps at the start of the hand.

PROBLEM 3

```
        ♠ Q 9 6 5
        ♡ A Q 6
        ◇ Q 9
        ♣ 8 7 4 3
```

♣Q led

```
        ┌─────────┐
        │         │
        └─────────┘
```

```
        ♠ K J 10 8 7 4 3
        ♡ K 5
        ◇ 10 6
        ♣ A 9
```

West	North	East	South
			1♠
pass	3♠	pass	4♠
all pass			

When South opens 1♠, North is worth a raise to 3♠. Although South holds only 11 high-card points, his seven-card trump suit justifies going on to game. What plan will you make when West leads the ♣Q?

You will remember that you should draw trumps immediately unless there is a good reason not to do so. What will happen if you win with the ♣A and play a trump at Trick 2? It's not difficult to see the answer. The defenders will win with the ♠A, say 'Thank you very much' and score three winners in clubs and diamonds. You will go one down.

There is a better way to proceed instead of playing like that. Yes, that's right. You should make a plan!

When you count the losers in the South hand, you see that there is one in spades and none in hearts, since dummy's ace covers the loser in your hand. You have two diamond losers and one in clubs. This is the loser summary:

Losers: ♠ 1   ♡ 0   ◇ 2   ♣ 1   Total: 4

How can you reduce this total to three losers? We have already seen that leading a trump is not a good idea. What will you do instead?

POINT TO REMEMBER

On this deal you have two 'quick losers' in the diamond suit – the defenders can score tricks there immediately if they win the lead. It will sometimes be right to look for a way to avoid these losers (discarding at least one of them) before drawing trumps. This happens when the defenders hold a top trump and can win the lead if you play trumps first. On this deal you also have a quick loser in clubs after West's club lead.

SOLUTION 3

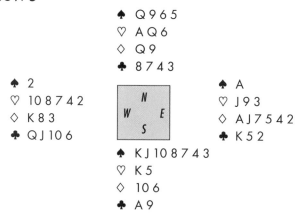

```
              ♠ Q 9 6 5
              ♡ A Q 6
              ◇ Q 9
              ♣ 8 7 4 3

♠ 2                          ♠ A
♡ 10 8 7 4 2      N          ♡ J 9 3
◇ K 8 3       W      E       ◇ A J 7 5 4 2
♣ Q J 10 6        S          ♣ K 5 2

              ♠ K J 10 8 7 4 3
              ♡ K 5
              ◇ 10 6
              ♣ A 9
```

West leads the ♣Q against your spade game and this is the loser position:

Losers: ♠ 1   ♡ 0   ◇ 2   ♣ 1   Total: 4

You have only two hearts in your hand and a total of three top heart winners. You can therefore discard a loser from the South hand on dummy's surplus heart winner. What is more, you must do this immediately, before drawing trumps.

Why is that? If you play a trump, the defenders will win the trick and be able to score three further tricks before you've had a chance to discard one of your losers.

So, you win the first trick with the ♣A and turn to the heart suit straight away. You play the ♡K first (following the general rule of playing the high card from the short side first). You then cross to the dummy's ♡A and play the ♡Q, discarding a club (or a diamond).

With this important task behind you, it is time to draw trumps. When East wins with the ♠A the defenders will no longer be able to score three minor-suit tricks. You discarded your remaining club so they can score only two more tricks, and you will make the contract.

> **PLAN: I will win with the ♣A and play three heart winners immediately, discarding a club. Only then will I draw trumps.**

POINT TO REMEMBER

One reason not to draw trumps immediately is that you need to discard one or more quick losers first. This happens when the defenders may win the first round of trumps (with the ace or king) and could then score enough tricks to eventually beat the contract.

PROBLEM 4

◇Q led

```
        ♠ 9 8 5 2
        ♡ J 9 8 6
        ◇ A 7 3
        ♣ Q 6

        ┌─────────┐
        │         │
        └─────────┘

        ♠ K 4
        ♡ A K Q 7 3
        ◇ 9 8 6
        ♣ A K 8
```

West	North	East	South
			1♡
pass	2♡	pass	4♡
all pass			

You open 1♡ on your 19 HCP, intending to carry the bidding to game (at least) if partner responds. When partner raises hearts to the two-level, you bid game in that suit.

How do you rate your chances when West leads the ◇Q? You may intend to win the first trick with dummy's ◇A, but it is good discipline to make a plan before you play the first card from dummy. You are in a suit contract, so the first step is to count the losers in each suit. You have two possible losers in spades and none in hearts. You have three diamonds in your hand and only one of these is covered by dummy's ace. That leaves you with two diamond losers. In clubs you have no losers because your third club is covered by dummy's ♣Q.

This is the loser position:

Losers: ♠ 2   ♡ 0   ◇ 2   ♣ 0   Total: 4

How can you reduce this total to three losers? One possible chance is to lead towards the ♠K, hoping that East holds the ♠A. If nothing better was available, you might have to do that. You would be relying on good luck, however, and no one likes to do that (particularly unlucky players!)

Can you see how to make the contract without relying on luck at all?

SOLUTION 4

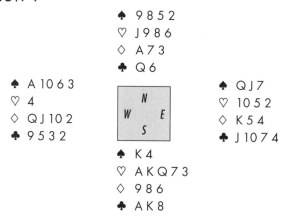

```
              ♠ 9 8 5 2
              ♡ J 9 8 6
              ◇ A 7 3
              ♣ Q 6
♠ A 10 6 3                      ♠ Q J 7
♡ 4              N              ♡ 10 5 2
◇ Q J 10 2   W       E          ◇ K 5 4
♣ 9 5 3 2        S              ♣ J 10 7 4
              ♠ K 4
              ♡ A K Q 7 3
              ◇ 9 8 6
              ♣ A K 8
```

West leads the ◇Q against your heart game and this is the loser position:

Losers: ♠ 2   ♡ 0   ◇ 2   ♣ 0   Total: 4

To avoid one of your spade losers, you could lead towards the ♠K, hoping that East held the ♠A. That would rely on good luck. Suppose you win the first trick with the ◇A, draw trumps and lead towards the ♠K. West will win with the ♠A and the defenders will score two diamond tricks and one more spade — one down.

A better idea is to discard a diamond loser. In the deals we have seen so far, dummy held a surplus winner in one of the side suits and this allowed you to discard a loser from your hand. Here the situation is different. You have a surplus club winner in your hand and can discard a diamond loser from dummy. It will work just as well! After discarding one of dummy's diamonds, you will have one diamond in dummy and two in your hand; you will be able to ruff your third diamond in the dummy, losing only one diamond trick. How does the play go?

You win the first trick with the ◇A and draw trumps in three rounds. You then play the ♣Q (short side first), followed by the ♣A and ♣K. On the third round of clubs you throw one of dummy's two remaining diamonds. Next you lead a low diamond, giving the defenders a diamond trick. East wins and switches to the ♠Q. The defenders score two spades but when you regain the lead you will ruff your last diamond in the dummy and make the game.

> **PLAN: I will win with the ◇A and draw trumps. I will then play three club winners, throwing a diamond from dummy. I will then ruff my last diamond in dummy.**

POINT TO REMEMBER

Sometimes you can use a surplus winner in your hand to throw a loser from the dummy. This may allow you to ruff one of your losers in the dummy.

PROBLEM 5

♠ A 7 5
♡ K Q 4
◇ J 6 5
♣ Q 8 5 3

♠J led

♠ K 8 3
♡ J 7
◇ A K Q 10 9 7 2
♣ A

West	North	East	South
	1♣	pass	2◇
pass	2NT	pass	6◇
all pass			

You would have bid much better than that. Yes, we believe you! Anyway, how would you tackle the diamond slam when West leads the ♠J?

The fact that you are in a slam makes no difference to the way in which you plan the contract. The first step is to count the potential losers. You have one in spades, since dummy's ♠A covers one of your two losers. You have one loser in hearts, because the defenders will score the ♡A. There are no further losers in either diamonds or clubs. This is your loser situation:

Losers: ♠ 1   ♡ 1   ◇ 0   ♣ 0   Total: 2

You can hardly expect to avoid the heart loser, so you must look for a way to avoid the possible loser in spades. There are three basic ways to avoid a loser: ruffing, discarding and finessing. Can you ruff a spade in dummy? No. Can you take a finesse in spades? No. There is only one way of avoiding a loser left — you must discard it.

Do you see how this can be done?

SOLUTION 5

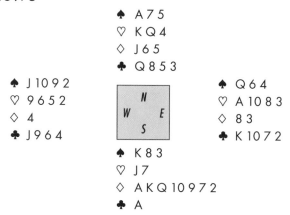

```
          ♠ A 7 5
          ♡ K Q 4
          ◇ J 6 5
          ♣ Q 8 5 3
♠ J 10 9 2              ♠ Q 6 4
♡ 9 6 5 2     N        ♡ A 10 8 3
◇ 4       W     E      ◇ 8 3
♣ J 9 6 4     S        ♣ K 10 7 2
          ♠ K 8 3
          ♡ J 7
          ◇ A K Q 10 9 7 2
          ♣ A
```

West leads the ♠J against your small slam in diamonds and this is the loser position:

Losers: ♠ 1   ♡ 1   ◇ 0   ♣ 0   Total: 2

You need to avoid the potential spade loser. The answer is to discard it on a surplus heart winner in dummy. At the moment dummy does not contain a surplus heart winner. You will need to knock out the defenders' ♡A to establish two heart winners in dummy. You will then be able to discard a spade on the third round of hearts. How does the play go?

You win the first trick with the ♠K and draw trumps in two rounds. You then lead the ♡J from your hand (following the general rule of starting with a high card from the short side). Let's say that East wins the first round of hearts and returns a spade. You win with dummy's ♠A and play the ♡K followed by the ♡Q. On the third round of hearts you discard a low spade from your hand. The contract is yours.

This is the first deal we have seen where a discard was not available immediately. You had to 'establish a suit' in dummy. Only then did you have a surplus winner on which you could take a discard.

Establishing a suit (in other words, creating some winners there) is such an important topic that we will have a whole chapter of quiz problems on it (Chapter 5).

> **PLAN: After drawing trumps, I will establish the heart suit. I will then be able to throw a spade loser on the third round of hearts.**

POINT TO REMEMBER

Quite often you need to establish (set up) a high card or two in dummy on which you can discard a loser from your hand. Usually you will draw trumps before doing this.

PROBLEM 6

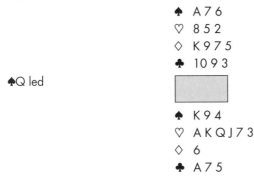

♠Q led

♠ A 7 6
♡ 8 5 2
◇ K 9 7 5
♣ 10 9 3

♠ K 9 4
♡ A K Q J 7 3
◇ 6
♣ A 7 5

West	North	East	South
			1♡
pass	2♡	pass	4♡
all pass			

When South hears a single raise, he decides that he is strong enough to bid 4♡. How would you tackle this contract when West leads the ♠Q?

If dummy had held the ♣K instead of the ◇K there would have been ten tricks on top — six trumps and two A-K combinations. Still, bridge would be an easy game if declarer were allowed to change the dummy a bit before playing the contract. What plan will you make?

You have one loser in spades and none in hearts, the trump suit. One loser in diamonds is accompanied by two more losers in clubs. This is the loser summary:

Losers: ♠ 1   ♡ 0   ◇ 1   ♣ 2   Total: 4

Can you see any chance of making the contract? You might try leading your singleton diamond, hoping that West holds the ◇A and decides to play low. Dummy's ◇K would win and you would no longer have a diamond loser. Is hoping for a defensive error your only chance?

SOLUTION 6

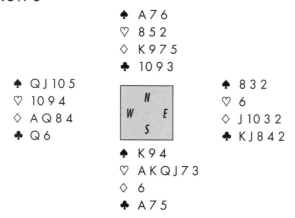

```
              ♠ A 7 6
              ♡ 8 5 2
              ◇ K 9 7 5
              ♣ 10 9 3

♠ Q J 10 5         N          ♠ 8 3 2
♡ 10 9 4      W         E     ♡ 6
◇ A Q 8 4          S          ◇ J 10 3 2
♣ Q 6                         ♣ K J 8 4 2

              ♠ K 9 4
              ♡ A K Q J 7 3
              ◇ 6
              ♣ A 7 5
```

West leads the ♠Q against your heart game and this is the loser position:

Losers: ♠ 1 ♡ 0 ◇ 1 ♣ 2   Total: 4

You are missing the ◇A and must hope to avoid three further losers in the black suits by discarding a spade or a club. How can you establish a surplus winner in dummy, which will provide a discard?

    The only chance is to lead a diamond towards the king, hoping that West holds the ◇A. If so, you will make the contract no matter what West does. Suppose that West rises with the ◇A when you lead your singleton diamond. This will set up the ◇K as a surplus winner in dummy. Provided you have an entry to dummy, you will then be able to cross to dummy and discard a loser on the ◇K.

    How does the play go? The deal is a good example of why you should always make a plan before playing to the first trick. Since you may need an entry to dummy, to reach the ◇K, it is essential to win the first trick with the ♠K. By doing so, you will preserve dummy's ♠A as an entry for later in the play. You draw trumps in three rounds and then lead the ◇6.

    It makes no difference what West decides to do. If he plays low, dummy's ◇K will win and you will have no diamond loser. If instead West rises with the ◇A, you can win his return and use the ♠A as an entry to play dummy's ◇K, discarding a spade or a club from your hand.

> **PLAN: I will win with the ♠K, draw trumps and lead towards the ◇K, hoping to set up a discard for one of my losers.**

POINT TO REMEMBER

You can often score a trick with an honor that is not a master (a top card) by leading towards it. By leading a singleton towards a king in dummy, you may be able to establish the king and discard a loser on it later.

PROBLEM 7

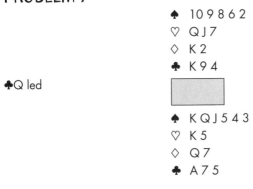

♠ 10 9 8 6 2
♡ Q J 7
◇ K 2
♣ K 9 4

♣Q led

♠ K Q J 5 4 3
♡ K 5
◇ Q 7
♣ A 7 5

West	North	East	South
			1♠
pass	4♠	all pass	

North's raise to game shows a fairly weak hand with five-card spade support. Some bridge teachers call this type of hand a 'weak freak'. What is your plan for the contract when West leads the ♣Q?

You will be familiar by now with the first step of making a plan for a suit contract — counting the possible losers in each suit. Here you have one spade loser, to the ace. It's the same in both hearts and diamonds, where you will lose to the defenders' ace. In clubs you have one possible loser on the third round. You start with this position:

Losers: ♠ 1   ♡ 1   ◇ 1   ♣ 1   Total: 4

There is no hope of avoiding the losers in spades, hearts and diamonds. You will therefore have to find a way to avoid the club loser. Do you have any ideas?

SOLUTION 7

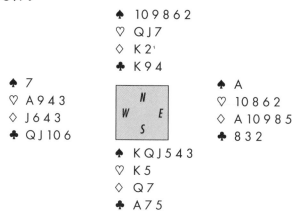

```
            ♠ 10 9 8 6 2
            ♡ Q J 7
            ◇ K 2
            ♣ K 9 4
♠ 7                           ♠ A
♡ A 9 4 3         N           ♡ 10 8 6 2
◇ J 6 4 3     W       E       ◇ A 10 9 8 5
♣ Q J 10 6        S           ♣ 8 3 2
            ♠ K Q J 5 4 3
            ♡ K 5
            ◇ Q 7
            ♣ A 7 5
```

West leads the ♣Q against your spade game and this is the loser position:

Losers: ♠ 1 ♡ 1 ◇ 1 ♣ 1 Total: 4

You will need to avoid a loser in clubs and this can be done by discarding a club on the surplus heart winner in dummy (after hearts have been established).

This deal is a little more difficult than some of the others and you will need to make a careful plan. What will happen if you win the club lead and play a trump? East will win with the ♠A and return a club, removing your last stopper in the suit. You will then go down! You can establish a surplus winner in hearts, yes, but it will be too late. The defenders will score a club trick when they win with the ♡A. You will lose a trick in each suit, going one down.

This is another deal where there is a good reason not to draw trumps straight away. It is more important to lead the ♡K, setting up the heart suit for a club discard. Let's say that West wins with the ♡A and plays another club. You win in the dummy and play the ♡Q and ♡J, discarding your club loser. You can then draw trumps and make the contract easily.

> **PLAN: I will win the club lead with the ace and lead the ♡K (setting up hearts immediately, before drawing trumps). I will then discard my club loser on the surplus heart winner. After drawing trumps, I will set up a winner in diamonds.**

POINT TO REMEMBER

One reason not to draw trumps immediately is that the defenders hold a top trump and you need to establish a side suit for discards. If you mistakenly play a trump first, they will win and remove your last stopper in the suit that they led.

PROBLEM 8

♠ 6 5 2
♡ A 9 2
◇ 8 6 3
♣ A J 10 6

♡K led

♠ A K Q 8 7
♡ 8 7 4
◇ A 10
♣ K Q 3

West	North	East	South
			1♠
pass	2♠	pass	4♠
all pass			

North raises to 2♠ and you are happy to bid game. What is your plan when West leads the ♡K?

Before winning with dummy's ♡A, you pause to count the losers in the long-trump (South) hand. You are hoping for no losers in the spade suit, but a 4-1 trump break would leave you with one loser there. You have two losers in hearts and one in diamonds. The club suit is solid, with no losers. You start with this loser position:

Losers: ♠ 1 (or 0) ♡ 2 ◇ 1 ♣ 0 **Total: 4**

Since there will be no problem if trumps break 3-2 (you would have a total of only three potential losers), you should make a plan on the assumption that there will be a trump loser. In that case you will have to dispose of one of your red-suit losers.

You have a surplus winner in clubs, which could allow you to discard a loser. Can you see any possible problem that may arise during the play? How will you play the contract?

SOLUTION 8

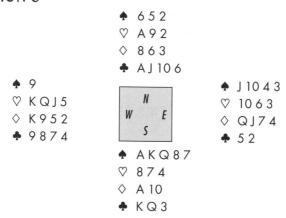

```
            ♠ 6 5 2
            ♡ A 9 2
            ◇ 8 6 3
            ♣ A J 10 6
♠ 9                          ♠ J 10 4 3
♡ K Q J 5        N           ♡ 10 6 3
◇ K 9 5 2    W       E       ◇ Q J 7 4
♣ 9 8 7 4        S           ♣ 5 2
            ♠ A K Q 8 7
            ♡ 8 7 4
            ◇ A 10
            ♣ K Q 3
```

West leads the ♡K against your spade game and this is the loser position:

Losers: ♠ 1 (or 0)   ♡ 2   ◇ 1   ♣ 0   Total: 4

If the defenders' trumps break 3-2, nothing can stop you from scoring five trumps, four clubs and the two red aces for an overtrick. You should therefore worry about trumps being 4-1. In that case you will have a trump loser, giving you a total of four losers. How can you avoid one of your potential losers in the red suits?

You have a surplus winner in clubs and can discard the ◇10 on the fourth round of clubs. There is a trap on this deal, though, and you must plan the play carefully. You win with the ♡A and play the ♠A and ♠K, West showing out on the second round. Suppose you play the ♠Q next and then start to play the clubs. Can you see what will happen?

Disaster! East will ruff the third round of clubs with his master ♠J. There is no entry to return to dummy. With no chance to discard a loser, you will lose three further tricks in the red suits and go down. Can you see how to avoid this?

After playing three rounds of trumps, you must remove East's master trump (the ♠J) by leading a low trump from your hand. East wins with the ♠J and the defenders score two heart tricks. When they switch to a diamond, you will win the trick and play four rounds of clubs, throwing your ◇10.

> **PLAN: I will win the heart lead and draw three rounds of trumps. If they break 4-1, I will give up a trump trick to the defenders. When I regain the lead, I will be able to play four rounds of clubs and discard the ◇10.**

POINT TO REMEMBER

You should draw a master trump held by a defender only if the defender could use the trump to stop you enjoying some winners in the dummy.

PROBLEM 9

♠ J 5 2
♡ A Q 8 2
◊ J 6 3
♣ 9 7 6

◊A led

♠ A K Q 10 7
♡ K 7 4
◊ 10 9 2
♣ A Q

West	North	East	South
			1♠
pass	2♠	pass	4♠
all pass			

You reach a game in spades and West leads the ◊A, followed by the ◊K and ◊Q. East follows to all three rounds and West then switches to a low trump. How will you play the contract?

You have already lost the three tricks that you can afford to lose. You need to make a plan to avoid any further loser. You started with no losers in spades or hearts. In diamonds you had three immediate losers (as the defenders have just demonstrated). There is one further potential loser in clubs. This was your starting position:

Losers: ♠ 0   ♡ 0   ◊ 3   ♣ 1   Total: 4

Three diamond tricks are already lost, so you must try to avoid a club loser. How many different chances can you see of doing this?

SOLUTION 9

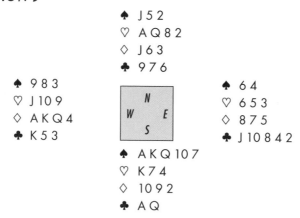

```
                    ♠ J 5 2
                    ♡ A Q 8 2
                    ◊ J 6 3
                    ♣ 9 7 6
   ♠ 9 8 3                          ♠ 6 4
   ♡ J 10 9          N              ♡ 6 5 3
   ◊ A K Q 4     W       E          ◊ 8 7 5
   ♣ K 5 3          S              ♣ J 10 8 4 2
                    ♠ A K Q 10 7
                    ♡ K 7 4
                    ◊ 10 9 2
                    ♣ A Q
```

West leads the ◊A against your spade game and this is the loser position:

Losers: ♠ 0   ♡ 0   ◊ 3   ♣ 1   Total: 4

West plays two more diamond winners, East following all the while, and you must look for a way to avoid a club loser. Any ideas?

One possible chance is to finesse the ♣Q (in other words, to lead a low club to the queen, hoping that East holds the king). If East holds the ♣K, you will be lucky; you will not lose a club trick and will make the game. This relies on luck, of course. Do you see any other possible way of avoiding a club loser?

Look at the heart suit. The defenders hold six missing hearts. If hearts break 3-3, dummy's last heart will become a surplus winner! You will be able to discard the ♣Q on it. If hearts do not break 3-3, you can take your remaining chance, a finesse of the ♣Q. How should you play the hand to combine both chances?

You win West's trump switch at Trick 4 and draw the remaining trumps. You then play the ♡K, followed by the ♡A and ♡Q. When you do this, both defenders follow all the way. Dummy's last heart, the ♡8, is now a winner (because neither defender has a heart left). You lead it and discard the ♣Q. The game is yours. If hearts had not broken 3-3, you would have taken the club finesse, hoping that East held the ♣K.

> **PLAN: I will draw trumps and play the ♡K, ♡A and ♡Q. If hearts break 3-3, I will discard the ♣Q on dummy's last heart. If hearts do not break, I will have to take the club finesse.**

POINT TO REMEMBER

Sometimes it is possible to combine two chances of making the contract.
Here you combined the chance of hearts breaking 3-3 (which would permit a club discard) with the chance of the club finesse being successful.

PROBLEM 10

♠ K 5 2
♡ 9 7
◇ A K 6 3
♣ A K Q 5

♠9 led

♠ A Q J 10 7
♡ K 5
◇ Q 8 2
♣ 8 7 4

West	North	East	South
			1♠
pass	2♣	pass	2NT
pass	6♠	all pass	

This is a quizbook on play, so we will keep the bidding simple! How will you play the small slam in spades when West leads the ♠9?

You pause to count your losers and see that you have no losers in spades, diamond or clubs. Your sole potential losers are two in the heart suit:

Losers: ♠ 0 ♡ 2 ◇ 0 ♣ 0 **Total:** 2

If you look at the heart suit on its own, you will see that you might avoid a heart loser by leading a heart from dummy towards the king. If you were lucky and East held the ♡A, you would make a trick with the ♡K and lose only one heart trick. When you are hoping to make a trick with an honor card that is not a master (the defenders hold one higher card), it is usually right to lead towards the honor. We will see several examples of this in Chapter 4 on Finesses.

However, perhaps you can somehow manage to discard one of your hearts. What plan will you make?

SOLUTION 10

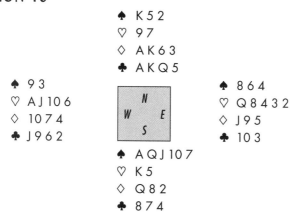

```
              ♠ K 5 2
              ♡ 9 7
              ◇ A K 6 3
              ♣ A K Q 5
♠ 9 3                        ♠ 8 6 4
♡ A J 10 6        N          ♡ Q 8 4 3 2
◇ 10 7 4      W     E        ◇ J 9 5
♣ J 9 6 2        S           ♣ 10 3
              ♠ A Q J 10 7
              ♡ K 5
              ◇ Q 8 2
              ♣ 8 7 4
```

West leads the ♠9 against your contract of 6♠. This is the loser position:

Losers: ♠ 0   ♡ 2   ◇ 0   ♣ 0   Total: 2

If possible, you would like to discard one of your hearts on a surplus winner in the dummy. What will you need to happen in order for a surplus winner in clubs to become available for a discard?

You will need the defenders' six clubs to break 3-3. If they both follow to the first three rounds of clubs, dummy's lowly ♣5 will be good. Neither defender will have any clubs left and you will be able to discard one of your heart losers.

Now look at the diamond suit. What will you need to happen for a discard to be available on the diamond suit?

The answer is the same. You will need the defenders' six diamonds to break 3-3. Dummy's ◇6 will then become good and you will be able to discard one of your heart losers. How does the play go?

You win the trump lead and draw trumps in two further rounds. You must now test one of the minor suits to see if it breaks 3-3 and will provide you with a discard. Let's say that you play the ♣A, ♣K and ♣Q. No luck there! East shows out on the third round and West's ♣J will prevent dummy's last club from scoring.

Next you play the ◇Q, ◇A and ◇K. That's better! Both defenders follow all the way and dummy's ◇6 is then good. You lead that card, throwing the ♡5, and slam is yours. If neither minor had broken 3-3, you would have taken your last chance, leading towards the ♡K.

> **PLAN: I will draw trumps and play the ♣AKQ. If clubs break 3-3, I will discard a heart on the good club. If not, I will play the ◇Q, ◇A and ◇K. If diamonds break 3-3, I'll discard a heart on the last diamond. Otherwise I must lead towards the ♡K, hoping that East has the ♡A.**

3

RUFFING LOSERS

In this chapter you can test yourself on several contracts that can be made by ruffing one or more losers in the hand with the fewer trumps (usually the dummy). For each problem, as always, you should start by making a plan. This will involve counting your potential losers and then seeing how you can reduce this number to allow you to make the contract. After forming a general plan, you must decide the order of play. As in the previous chapter, this will usually involve drawing trumps immediately unless there is some good reason not to.

Before the first problem, let's look at the general idea of creating an extra trick by ruffing. Suppose that you are in 4♠ and this is your trump suit:

If you simply draw trumps, you will score six trump tricks. What will happen if dummy is short in one of the side suits and you can take a ruff with the ♠2? How many trump tricks will you score then?

Seven, yes. You will score six trump tricks in the long-trump (South) hand and one ruffing trick in the dummy.

Now suppose that there is a shortage in declarer's hand, the one with six trumps. What will happen if you take a ruff there, with the ♠6? You will not score an extra trick! The ♠6 was going to give you a sixth trump trick already. You gain nothing by ruffing in the long-trump hand.

POINT TO REMEMBER

A ruff in the short-trump hand gives you an extra trick. A ruff in the long-trump hand does not.

Let's put that trump suit into a full deal and see how you might make a plan for the small slam contract on the next page.

```
                    ♠ 7 5 2
                    ♡ 9 4
                    ◇ A 10 7 6 2
                    ♣ 10 8 5
    ♠ J 4                          ♠ 10 3
    ♡ 10 7 5 3          N          ♡ Q J 8 2
    ◇ K Q J 4      W       E       ◇ 9 8 3
    ♣ 9 6 3            S           ♣ A 7 4 2
                    ♠ A K Q 9 8 6
                    ♡ A K 6
                    ◇ 5
                    ♣ K Q J
```

West	North	East	South
			2♣
pass	2◇	pass	2♠
pass	3♠	pass	4NT
pass	5◇	pass	6♠
all pass			

How will you play 6♠ when West leads the ◇K?

As always in a suit contract, you start by counting your losers. You have no losers in the trump suit (unless trumps break 4-0, but then you will go down anyway). In hearts you have one loser. Your diamond singleton is covered by dummy's ◇A. In clubs you have one loser to the ace. This is the position:

Losers: ♠ 0   ♡ 1   ◇ 0   ♣ 1   Total: 2

You are certain to lose a club trick, so you must avoid losing a heart trick. How can this be done?

Dummy has only two hearts, so you can ruff the ♡6 on the third round of the suit. How does the play go?

You win the diamond lead with dummy's ace. Is there any point in ruffing a diamond in the long-trump hand now? No, because it will not give you an extra trick. Your objective is to take a ruff in the short-trump hand, ruffing a heart.

Before doing this, you should play the ♠A and ♠K, drawing two rounds of trumps. (If one of the defenders holds a doubleton heart, this may stop him from ruffing with a higher trump than the dummy.) As it happens, trumps break 2-2. You play the ♡A and ♡K and lead the ♡6, ruffing with dummy's last trump. You then play clubs, setting up two tricks there.

> **PLAN: I will win the diamond lead and draw two rounds of trumps. I will then play the two top hearts and ruff a heart in the dummy. Finally, I will set up two tricks in the club suit.**

PROBLEM 11

```
        ♠ 7 2
        ♡ J 9 4
        ◇ K 2
        ♣ A 8 6 5 3 2
♣Q led
        ┌─────────┐
        │         │
        └─────────┘
        ♠ A K Q J 10 4
        ♡ 8 6 5
        ◇ A 8 4
        ♣ 4
```

West	North	East	South
			1♠
pass	1NT	pass	3♠
pass	4♠		
all pass			

What is your plan for the contract when West leads the ♣Q?

You have no spade loser and three heart losers. You have one diamond loser (dummy's ◇K covers one of your low cards) and no loser in clubs. You start with this position:

Losers: ♠ 0   ♡ 3   ◇ 1   ♣ 0   Total: 4

There is little prospect of avoiding the three losers in hearts. How can you prevent the defenders from scoring a diamond trick? Dummy has only two diamonds to your three, so you will have a chance to ruff a diamond in dummy. This will give you an extra trick as well as avoiding a loser.

What is your plan for making the spade game? How will you play the contract?

SOLUTION 11

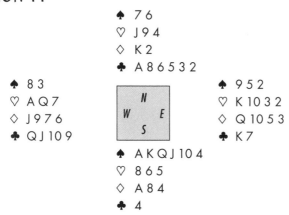

```
              ♠ 7 6
              ♡ J 9 4
              ◇ K 2
              ♣ A 8 6 5 3 2
♠ 8 3                          ♠ 9 5 2
♡ A Q 7          N              ♡ K 10 3 2
◇ J 9 7 6    W       E         ◇ Q 10 5 3
♣ Q J 10 9       S             ♣ K 7
              ♠ A K Q J 10 4
              ♡ 8 6 5
              ◇ A 8 4
              ♣ 4
```

West leads the ♣Q against your spade game and this is the loser position:

Losers: ♠ 0 ♡ 3 ◇ 1 ♣ 0 Total: 4

You can avoid the loser in diamonds by ruffing (trumping) the third round of diamonds in the dummy. How will you play the contract? After winning the ♣Q lead with the ♣A, should you draw trumps?

No! You need to ruff a diamond in the dummy. This will be impossible if you have drawn trumps and dummy does not have any trumps left. After winning the club lead in dummy, you should lead the ◇K (the high card from the short side first). You continue with the ◇2 to your ◇A. You are then in the right hand to lead a third round of diamonds. You ruff with one of dummy's trumps and both defenders follow suit.

With this important piece of work behind you, lead dummy's remaining trump to your hand and draw trumps. You will make the contract, losing just three heart tricks at the end.

> **PLAN: I will win the club lead, play the ◇K and ◇A and ruff the third round of diamonds in the dummy. I will then draw trumps.**

Although we have been concentrating on reducing the number of losers when planning the contracts, let's look now at the tricks that you won. You started with nine top tricks: six trumps, the ◇AK and the ♣A. By ruffing a diamond in the shorter trump holding, you added one extra trick, bringing the total to ten.

POINT TO REMEMBER _____

One reason not to draw trumps immediately is that you may need dummy's trumps to ruff one or more of your losers.

PROBLEM 12

♠ 10 5 2
♡ A 3
♢ A 8 5
♣ 9 7 5 4 2

◇K led

♠ A K Q J 6
♡ K 9 7
♢ 10 9 3
♣ K Q

West	North	East	South
			1♠
pass	2♠	pass	4♠
all pass			

Since your 1♠ opening bid promises at least five cards in the suit, North is happy to raise to 2♠. Expecting there to be good play for ten tricks, you jump to the spade game. What is your plan for this contract when West leads the ◇K?

You have no losers in spades. In hearts you have one loser. You have three hearts in your hand and dummy's ♡A covers one of your two low hearts. In diamonds you have two losers and in clubs you have one loser, to the ace. This is a summary of your loser situation:

Losers: ♠ 0   ♡ 1   ♢ 2   ♣ 1   Total: 4

You must somehow reduce the number of losers from four to three. How will you do this?

SOLUTION 12

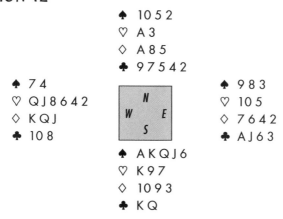

```
              ♠ 10 5 2
              ♡ A 3
              ◇ A 8 5
              ♣ 9 7 5 4 2
♠ 7 4                        ♠ 9 8 3
♡ Q J 8 6 4 2      N         ♡ 10 5
◇ K Q J       W        E     ◇ 7 6 4 2
♣ 10 8             S         ♣ A J 6 3
              ♠ A K Q J 6
              ♡ K 9 7
              ◇ 10 9 3
              ♣ K Q
```

West leads the ◇K against your spade game. Before playing a card from dummy, you must make a plan. You start with these potential losers:

Losers: ♠ 0   ♡ 1   ◇ 2   ♣ 1   Total: 4

It is unlikely that you can avoid any of the three minor-suit losers. In hearts you have a good chance of avoiding a loser by ruffing the third round of hearts in the dummy. How does the play go?

You win the diamond lead with the ace and must now decide whether to draw trumps straight away. What would happen if you drew three rounds of trumps? You would have no trump left in dummy and would not be able to ruff a heart.

At Trick 2 you should play one round of trumps, leading low to your ace. When both defenders follow to this trick, you know that trumps are not 5-0. You play the ♡7 to the ♡A (winning the first round with the high card in the shorter holding). You then play the ♡3 to your ♡K and lead a third round of hearts. Will you ruff with the ♠10 or the ♠5?

Since you have plenty of high trumps, you can afford to ruff the heart with a master trump, the ♠10. This will avoid any risk that East can overruff. It's just as well that you took this precaution! East is out of hearts but cannot overruff the ♠10. You draw trumps and eventually set up a club trick to bring your total to ten.

> **PLAN: I will win the diamond lead and draw one round of trumps with the ace. I will then play the ♡A and ♡K. When I lead a third round of hearts, I will ruff with dummy's ♠10 to avoid any chance of an overruff. I can then draw trumps.**

POINT TO REMEMBER

You can afford to ruff high (with an honor) if you will still have enough trump honors to draw the defenders' trumps.

PROBLEM 13

          ♠ A K 10 5
          ♡ K 7 4
          ◇ J 7 6 2
          ♣ J 5

◇A led

          ♠ 6 4
          ♡ A Q J 10 5 3
          ◇ 9 5
          ♣ A 8 3

West	North	East	South
			1♡
pass	1♠	pass	2♡
pass	4♡	all pass	

What is your plan for this contract when West leads the ◇A?

You have no spade losers because your two cards are covered by dummy's ace and king. Nor do you have any losers in hearts. There are two losers in diamonds and a further two losers in clubs. This is the position:

Losers: ♠ 0 ♡ 0 ◇ 2 ♣ 2 Total: 4

The defenders will doubtless take their two diamond tricks. You must then try to reduce the number of club losers from two to one. How do you plan to do this?

SOLUTION 13

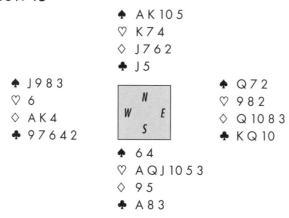

```
              ♠ A K 10 5
              ♡ K 7 4
              ◇ J 7 6 2
              ♣ J 5
♠ J 9 8 3                        ♠ Q 7 2
♡ 6              N               ♡ 9 8 2
◇ A K 4      W       E           ◇ Q 10 8 3
♣ 9 7 6 4 2      S               ♣ K Q 10
              ♠ 6 4
              ♡ A Q J 10 5 3
              ◇ 9 5
              ♣ A 8 3
```

West leads the ◇A against your heart game, continuing with the ◇K and a low diamond to East's ◇10. You ruff the third round of diamonds in your hand and observe this loser position:

Losers: ♠ 0   ♡ 0   ◇ 2   ♣ 2   Total: 4

You need to reduce the number of club losers from two to one. This can be done by ruffing the third round of clubs in the dummy. Your first decision is whether to draw trumps immediately. Three rounds of trumps would leave no trumps in the dummy; you would be unable to ruff a club.

Perhaps it seems a good idea to draw two rounds of trumps at the start, leaving one trump in dummy for a club ruff. The trouble with that approach is that you will have to give up a club trick before you can ruff the third round. When East wins his club trick he will be able to play a third round of trumps, depriving you of your ruff in the dummy.

After ruffing the third round of diamonds, you should play the ♣A and then lead another club, which East will win. Let's say that East returns a trump. You win with the ♡A and then ruff the third round of clubs with dummy's ♡K (to make sure that East cannot overruff). You can then draw trumps and make the remaining tricks.

> **PLAN: I will ruff the third diamond and play ace and another club. I can then ruff the third round of clubs with the ♡K and draw trumps.**

POINT TO REMEMBER

Sometimes you have to give up a trick in a suit before you can ruff a loser. Make sure that the defenders will have no chance to draw dummy's last trump when you do this.

PROBLEM 14

♠ A 6 5
♡ J 9 7 3
◇ 8 6
♣ 10 6 4 2

♠8 led

♠ K Q J 10 2
♡ A 8
◇ A K 7 2
♣ A K

West	North	East	South
			2♣
pass	2◇	pass	2♠
pass	3♠	pass	4NT
pass	5◇	pass	6♠
all pass			

You bid boldly to a small slam in spades and West leads the ♠8. How will you plan the contract?

You have no losers in spades and one in hearts. In diamonds, the ◇7 and ◇2 are potential losers. Your rock-solid ♣AK means that you have no club losers. This is the loser summary:

Losers: ♠0   ♡1   ◇2   ♣0   Total: 3

You have three potential losers and must reduce this to just one. There is no realistic chance of avoiding a heart loser but perhaps you can avoid the two diamond losers. Do you see how this might be done?

By good fortune dummy holds only two diamonds. This gives you the possibility of ruffing your two diamond losers. What plan will you make?

SOLUTION 14

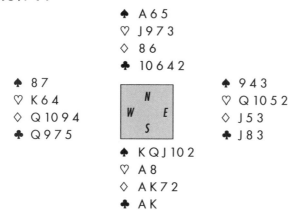

```
              ♠ A 6 5
              ♡ J 9 7 3
              ◇ 8 6
              ♣ 10 6 4 2
♠ 8 7                          ♠ 9 4 3
♡ K 6 4          N            ♡ Q 10 5 2
◇ Q 10 9 4    W     E         ◇ J 5 3
♣ Q 9 7 5        S            ♣ J 8 3
              ♠ K Q J 10 2
              ♡ A 8
              ◇ A K 7 2
              ♣ A K
```

West leads the ♠8 against your small slam in spades. You have these losers:

Losers: ♠ 0   ♡ 1   ◇ 2   ♣ 0   Total: 3

You have little chance of avoiding the loser in hearts and must aim to ruff your two diamond losers in the dummy. The lead leaves you with only two trumps in the dummy and both of these will be needed. Where should you win the opening lead?

Suppose you make the mistake of winning the opening lead with dummy's ♠A. You will then need to ruff the third and fourth rounds of diamonds with the ♠5 and ♠6. It is almost certain that one of the defenders (the one who has only three diamonds) will be able to ruff the fourth round with a higher trump.

Since you may need to ruff one of your diamond losers with a high trump, you should keep dummy's ♠A and win the trump lead in your hand. You cannot afford to draw any more trumps because both of dummy's trumps will be needed for ruffing. You play the ◇A and ◇K and then lead the ◇2, West following. Which of dummy's two remaining trumps (the ♠A and ♠6) should you use to ruff this trick?

You should ruff with the ♠6, using the low trump at a time when it is more likely that East will follow suit. After East does follow, you return to your hand with the ♣A and ruff your last diamond with the ♠A. You then cross back to the ♡A to draw the outstanding trumps. The slam is yours.

> **PLAN: I will win the trump lead in my hand and play the ◇A and ◇K. I will ruff one diamond with the ♠6 and then the other diamond with the ♠A. Finally, I will draw trumps.**

POINT TO REMEMBER

When you need to take two ruffs and have only one master trump with which to ruff, you should usually take the first ruff with a low trump, the second ruff with the top trump.

PROBLEM 15

♠ 9 8 7 5 2
♡ Q 7 5
◇ 8 3
♣ A 8 6

♠J led

♠ A 4
♡ A K J 10 9
◇ J 9 4
♣ K Q 3

West	North	East	South
			1♡
pass	2♡	pass	4♡
all pass			

A straightforward auction carries you to 4♡ and West leads the ♠J. What is your plan to land the game?

You start with one loser in spades and none in hearts, the trump suit. In diamonds you have three losers and the clubs are solid. This is the loser summary:

Losers: ♠ 1   ♡ 0   ◇ 3   ♣ 0   Total: 4

There is no real prospect of avoiding the spade loser, so you must try to reduce the number of diamond losers from three to two. Dummy has only two diamonds, so perhaps you can arrange a diamond ruff in dummy. What do you reckon?

If you think there may be a chance of taking a diamond ruff, what order of play do you have in mind?

SOLUTION 15

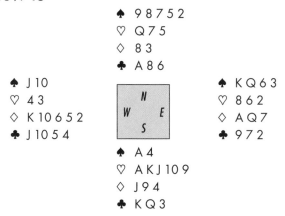

```
              ♠ 9 8 7 5 2
              ♡ Q 7 5
              ◇ 8 3
              ♣ A 8 6
♠ J 10                      ♠ K Q 6 3
♡ 4 3          N            ♡ 8 6 2
◇ K 10 6 5 2  W   E         ◇ A Q 7
♣ J 10 5 4        S         ♣ 9 7 2
              ♠ A 4
              ♡ A K J 10 9
              ◇ J 9 4
              ♣ K Q 3
```

West leads the ♠J against your heart game and this is the loser position:

Losers: ♠ 1   ♡ 0   ◇ 3   ♣ 0   Total: 4

You cannot avoid a spade loser and must seek to lose only two diamond tricks. This can be done if you can arrange a diamond ruff in dummy. Before that is possible, you will need to concede two diamond tricks to the defenders.

You win the spade lead and see that it would be a bad idea to draw even one round of trumps next. If you did, the defenders would play another round of trumps each time you surrendered a diamond trick. There would then be no trumps left in dummy to take your intended diamond ruff.

So, you give up a diamond trick at Trick 2, leading the ◇4. Let's say that East wins and returns a trump. You win with the ♡A and give up another diamond trick, leading the ◇9. The defenders win and play a second round of trumps. You win in your hand and ruff your last diamond with dummy's ♡Q. (You saved a top trump in dummy so that there would be no risk of a defender overruffing the third round of diamonds.)

You return to your hand with a club and draw the defenders' last trump. You will make the game with the loss of just one spade and two diamonds.

> **PLAN: I will win with the ♠A and give up a diamond trick. When I regain the lead I will give up a second diamond trick. I can then ruff my last diamond with the ♡Q and draw trumps.**

POINT TO REMEMBER

Quite often you have to give the defenders a trick or two in the suit that you are planning to ruff. Since they can lead trumps each time they win a trick, you must make sure that you will still have a trump left in the dummy.

PROBLEM 16

♠ K 4 3
♡ 8 6 5 4
◇ 5
♣ Q 8 7 4 2

♠9 led

♠ A Q 8 7 5
♡ A K
◇ A J 8
♣ 10 6 3

West	North	East	South
			1♠
pass	2♠	pass	4♠
all pass			

Despite holding only 5 HCP, North is easily worth a raise to 2♠. The singleton diamond means that declarer can probably score extra tricks by taking a ruff or two in the suit. How would you play this contract when West leads the ♠9?

Let's look at the club suit first. You have three club losers and not much chance of reducing that number. (If West held the ♣A and ♣K, which might allow you to set up the queen by leading clubs twice towards the dummy, he would probably have led the suit.) With three likely club losers, you will have to assume that the trumps break 3-2 and that there are no losers in the trump suit. You have two potential diamond losers, so this is the loser situation:

Losers: ♠ 0 ♡ 0 ◇ 2 ♣ 3 Total: 5

What is your plan for avoiding the two diamond losers? How will you play the hand?

POINT TO REMEMBER

When you need a favorable break in a suit to give you a chance of making the contract, make your plan on the assumption that the suit does break in this way. On this deal, you assume that the trumps will break 3-2.

SOLUTION 16

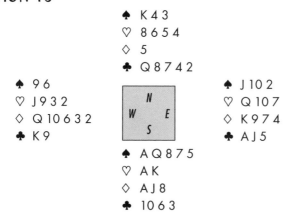

```
              ♠ K 4 3
              ♡ 8 6 5 4
              ◇ 5
              ♣ Q 8 7 4 2
♠ 9 6                        ♠ J 10 2
♡ J 9 3 2        N           ♡ Q 10 7
◇ Q 10 6 3 2   W   E         ◇ K 9 7 4
♣ K 9            S           ♣ A J 5
              ♠ A Q 8 7 5
              ♡ A K
              ◇ A J 8
              ♣ 10 6 3
```

West leads the ♠9 against your spade game. To give yourself a chance, you must assume that the trumps break 3-2 and that there will be no losers in the suit. This will then be the loser position:

Losers: ♠0 ♡0 ◇2 ♣3 Total: 5

How can you avoid the two diamond losers? Dummy holds only one diamond, so it seems that you can ruff the second and third rounds of the suit. Yes, but do you see a potential problem with that plan?

When this deal arose, the declarer won the trump lead with the queen in his hand and… could no longer make the contract! He could ruff his two diamonds in dummy, yes, but the second of those ruffs would have to be taken with the ♠K. With only the ace of trumps remaining to draw the opponents' three outstanding trumps, there would then be no way to prevent East's ♠J from scoring a trick.

Look at the trump position in the diagram above. The suit does break 3-2, which is what you need. To draw all the trumps, you will have to use the ace, king and queen. You must therefore use dummy's ♠4 and ♠3 to ruff your diamond losers. Do you see how you should play on the first trick?

You must win with dummy's ♠K. You cross to the ◇A and ruff a diamond with the ♠3. You return to your hand with the ♡K and ruff your last diamond with the ♠4. Next you play a heart to the ace, draw the outstanding trumps and the contract is yours. You will lose three club tricks but that is all.

> **PLAN: I will win the trump lead with the ♠K. I can then ruff my two losing diamonds with the ♠4 and ♠3.**

PROBLEM 17

♠ K J 3
♡ K 8
◇ 8 7 5 3 2
♣ 10 8 7

◇K led

♠ A Q 10 9 7 4
♡ 10 6 2
◇ A 6
♣ A K

West	North	East	South
			1♠
pass	2♠	pass	4♠
all pass			

How will you plan this contract when West leads the ◇K?

The trumps are solid and you have three potential losers in hearts. You have one loser in diamonds and no further losers in clubs. This is a summary of your losers:

Losers: ♠ 0   ♡ 3   ◇ 1   ♣ 0   Total: 4

You cannot hope to avoid the one loser in diamonds. What ways can you see of avoiding one or more heart losers? How will you play the hand to make the most of your chances?

SOLUTION 17

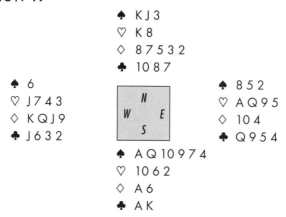

```
            ♠ K J 3
            ♡ K 8
            ◇ 8 7 5 3 2
            ♣ 10 8 7

♠ 6                          ♠ 8 5 2
♡ J 7 4 3      N             ♡ A Q 9 5
◇ K Q J 9   W     E          ◇ 10 4
♣ J 6 3 2      S             ♣ Q 9 5 4

            ♠ A Q 10 9 7 4
            ♡ 10 6 2
            ◇ A 6
            ♣ A K
```

West leads the ◇K against your spade game and this is the loser position:

Losers: ♠ 0   ♡ 3   ◇ 1   ♣ 0   Total: 4

Since you will surely lose a diamond trick, you must try to reduce the number of losers in hearts. One possibility is to lead towards the ♡K. If you are lucky and West holds the ♡A, you will make a trick with the king and cannot then lose more than two heart tricks. Whether or not West holds the ♡A, there is a chance that you can ruff your third heart in the dummy. You can afford to lose the first two heart tricks (when East holds the ♡A) provided you can then ruff your last heart.

The original declarer won the diamond lead with the ace and, without bothering to make a plan, drew one round of trumps with the ace. The contract could no longer be made! A heart to the king lost to the ace and East returned a second round of trumps. When declarer gave up a second round of hearts, East won and was able to play a third round of trumps. No heart ruff could be taken and the game was one down.

There was no reason at all to draw a round of trumps at the start. Had declarer paused to make a plan, he would have guaranteed a heart ruff in dummy by leading a heart to the king at Trick 2. East wins with the ace but cannot defeat the contract. Declarer can give up another heart and ruff the last heart in the dummy.

> **PLAN: I will win the diamond lead and play a heart to the king immediately. I can subsequently give up another heart and ruff a heart loser in dummy.**

POINT TO REMEMBER

Be wary of drawing any trumps when you need to give up a trick or two to set up a ruff in the dummy. The defenders may then be able to draw dummy's remaining trumps before you can take a ruff.

PROBLEM 18

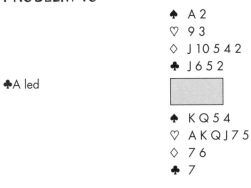

♠ A 2
♡ 9 3
◇ J 10 5 4 2
♣ J 6 5 2

♣A led

♠ K Q 5 4
♡ A K Q J 7 5
◇ 7 6
♣ 7

West	North	East	South
			1♡
pass	1NT	pass	4♡
all pass			

When North shows a few points with his 1NT response, you leap aggressively to 4♡. How will you play this contract when West leads the ♣A followed by the ♣K?

You ruff the second round of clubs and pause to count the losers in the long-trump (South) hand. Although you have the ♠AKQ between the hands, you still have a potential loser in spades on the fourth round. There are no losers in trumps. You have two losers in diamonds and one in clubs. This is the loser position:

Losers: ♠ 1 ♡ 0 ◇ 2 ♣ 1 **Total: 4**

You cannot avoid the three losers in the minor suits (clubs and diamonds). You must therefore make a plan to avoid the spade loser. How will you play the contract?

SOLUTION 18

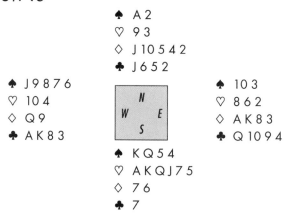

```
              ♠ A 2
              ♡ 9 3
              ◇ J 10 5 4 2
              ♣ J 6 5 2
♠ J 9 8 7 6                    ♠ 10 3
♡ 10 4          N             ♡ 8 6 2
◇ Q 9      W        E         ◇ A K 8 3
♣ A K 8 3        S            ♣ Q 10 9 4
              ♠ K Q 5 4
              ♡ A K Q J 7 5
              ◇ 7 6
              ♣ 7
```

Against your heart game, West leads the ♣A followed by the ♣K. You ruff the second club with the ♡5 and note this loser position:

Losers: ♠ 1   ♡ 0   ◇ 2   ♣ 1   Total: 4

You must aim to avoid the spade loser. Dummy has only two spades, so you have a chance to ruff a spade in dummy. How should the play go?

Drawing trumps straight away would not be a sensible idea because you would have no trump left in dummy to ruff your spade loser. You must attempt a spade ruff straight away. You lead a low spade to dummy's ace (playing the high card from the short side first, as usual). You then lead the ♠2 to the ♠K. What now?

There is no reason whatsoever to play the ♠Q next. Apart from such a play having no purpose, you would greatly increase the chance that one of the defenders would be able to ruff with the ♡10 when you subsequently led a fourth round of spades. When the cards lie as in the diagram, East would ruff the ♠Q. Not good!

So, at Trick 5 you lead the ♠5. West follows suit. Which trump will you use for ruffing, the ♡9 or ♡3? Most of the time East will have another spade and it will not matter. Here East began with only two spades, which was quite possible when he followed with the ♠10 on the second round. You should ruff with the ♡9 just in case East has no more spades but does not hold the ♡10. Yes, the plan works! East is out of spades but cannot overruff. You now draw trumps and make the contract.

> **PLAN: I will ruff the second club, play the ♠A and ♠K and ruff a low spade with dummy's ♡9. This will prevent an overruff when the defender short in spades does not hold the ♡10.**

POINT TO REMEMBER

Ruff with a master trump if you can afford it. Otherwise ruff with the highest trump available, to reduce the chance of an overruff.

PROBLEM 19

```
                    ♠ Q 7 2
                    ♡ Q 9 8 5 3 2
                    ◇ 7
                    ♣ K 8 2
♣J led
                    ┌─────────┐
                    │         │
                    └─────────┘
                    ♠ K J 10 9 8 3
                    ♡ 7
                    ◇ A 6 2
                    ♣ A 6 4
```

West	North	East	South
		1◇	1♠
3◇	3♠	pass	4♠
all pass			

You and your partner bid strongly to a game in spades. How will you plan to make this contract when West leads the ♣J?

You have one loser in spades, to the ace. In hearts you have one loser and in diamonds you have two losers. In clubs you have a slow loser on the third round. You start with this position:

Losers: ♠ 1   ♡ 1   ◇ 2   ♣ 1   Total: 5

You need to reduce the loser count from five to three. You may be able to ruff your two diamond losers in the dummy, but you will have to plan the play carefully to achieve this. Your first decision is this: 'Where should I win the first trick?'

SOLUTION 19

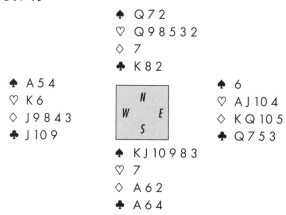

```
                        ♠ Q 7 2
                        ♡ Q 9 8 5 3 2
                        ◊ 7
                        ♣ K 8 2
     ♠ A 5 4                              ♠ 6
     ♡ K 6              ┌─────────┐       ♡ A J 10 4
     ◊ J 9 8 4 3       │    N    │       ◊ K Q 10 5
     ♣ J 10 9          │ W     E │       ♣ Q 7 5 3
                       │    S    │
                       └─────────┘
                        ♠ K J 10 9 8 3
                        ♡ 7
                        ◊ A 6 2
                        ♣ A 6 4
```

West leads the ♣J against your spade game and this is the loser position:

Losers: ♠ 1   ♡ 1   ◊ 2   ♣ 1   Total: 5

You must aim to ruff the two diamond losers. Suppose you do not make a proper plan and win the club lead in your hand. You play the ◊A and ruff a diamond in dummy. So far, so good. Oh dear, how can you reach your hand for a second diamond ruff? If you play a spade or a heart, the defenders will win and remove dummy's remaining trumps. You will go one down.

An important part of planning many bridge hands is to check that you have enough entries to carry out your intended line of play. Here you will need an entry to the South hand to ruff the second diamond. That entry has to be the ♣A. You should therefore win the first trick with dummy's ♣K. The rest of the play is then very easy indeed. Let's start at the beginning again.

You win the club lead with dummy's ♣K. You cross to the ◊A and ruff a diamond in dummy. You return to your hand with the ♣A and ruff your last diamond. You then draw trumps and make the contract.

> **PLAN: I will win the first trick with the ♣K, cross to the ◊A and ruff a diamond. I will return to the ♣A and ruff a diamond. Then I can draw trumps.**

POINT TO REMEMBER

One of the reasons to make a plan before playing to the first trick is that it may be important whether you win in dummy or in your hand. On this deal, and many others, you will go down if you win in the wrong hand.

PROBLEM 20 (a little more difficult)

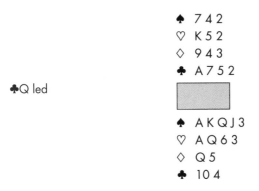

♠ 7 4 2
♡ K 5 2
♢ 9 4 3
♣ A 7 5 2

♣Q led

♠ A K Q J 3
♡ A Q 6 3
♢ Q 5
♣ 10 4

West	North	East	South
			1♠
pass	2♠	pass	4♠
all pass			

West leads the ♣Q against your spade game. What is your plan to make the contract?

You have no losers in spades (unless you are very unlucky and the suit breaks 5-0). In hearts you have a possible loser on the fourth round. You have two quick losers in diamonds and one slow loser in clubs. This is your loser position at the start:

Losers: ♠0   ♡1   ♢2   ♣1   Total: 4

Even a world champion could not prevent the three losers in the minor suits. What chances do you see of avoiding a heart loser? How will you play the hand?

SOLUTION 20

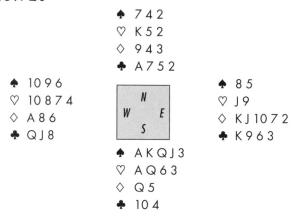

```
              ♠ 7 4 2
              ♡ K 5 2
              ◇ 9 4 3
              ♣ A 7 5 2
♠ 10 9 6                      ♠ 8 5
♡ 10 8 7 4      N            ♡ J 9
◇ A 8 6      W     E         ◇ K J 10 7 2
♣ Q J 8         S            ♣ K 9 6 3
              ♠ A K Q J 3
              ♡ A Q 6 3
              ◇ Q 5
              ♣ 10 4
```

West leads the ♣Q against your spade game and this is the loser position:

Losers: ♠0 ♡1 ◇2 ♣1 Total: 4

You must aim to avoid the heart loser. There are six hearts out. If the defenders' hearts divide 3-3, your ♡6 will become good after three rounds of the suit. Neither defender will then have a heart left. Is there any other way to avoid a heart loser?

It's not an easy play to find and some bridge players will play for many years without ever realizing that such contracts can be made! When the defenders' hearts split 4-2, you can still make the contract if the defender with the doubleton heart began with only two trumps.

You win the club lead and draw just two rounds of trumps, leaving one in the dummy. East began with a doubleton heart, but now has no trumps left. You play the ♡K and ♡A, both defenders following suit. Even though there is still a trump out, you must steel yourself to play the ♡Q next. Nothing will be lost if hearts are 3-3 (which is your main chance). In that case you would then draw the last trump.

When the cards lie as in the diagram, West follows to the ♡Q and East is unable to ruff. You ruff the fourth round of hearts in dummy and make the game.

> **PLAN: I will win the club lead and draw just two rounds of trumps. I will then play three top hearts. If hearts break 3-3, I will draw the last trump. When hearts break 4-2, I will still make the contract if the defender with two hearts has no more trumps left.**

POINT TO REMEMBER

If East can ruff the ♡Q, you will go one down — but you have not lost anything. In that case you could never make the contract. If you drew trumps before playing hearts, you would lose a heart trick at the end.

TAKING FINESSES

We have already seen two of the main ways in which you can reduce your initial number of losers — discarding and ruffing. We will now consider the third main method, which is finessing. What does that mean? It means trying to score a trick with a card (usually an honor) even though the defenders hold a higher honor. A simple example is when you lead a low card towards a king:

You start with two losers in this club suit. When West holds the ♣A, you can reduce this to one by leading towards dummy's ♣K. How does this work?

You lead the ♣4 from the South hand and West has to decide whether to play the ♣A or the ♣5. If he plays the ♣A ('rises with the ace', as players say), dummy's ♣K will score a trick on the second round of the suit. If instead West plays a low club, you will play the ♣K from dummy. This will win the trick because East does not hold the ♣A.

As you see, you rely on luck when you take a finesse. You hope that it will give you an extra trick but you cannot be sure.

The most important point to remember is that you lead towards the honor (the ♣K here). If you made the mistake of leading the ♣K or the ♣8 from dummy instead, you would lose two club tricks whichever defender held the ♣A.

Here is another basic example of the technique:

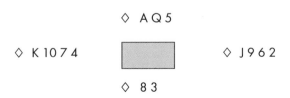

When you count your losers, making a plan for the contract, you see that you have one potential loser in diamonds. By taking a finesse, you will give yourself a chance of avoiding the loser. You lead the ◊3 from the South hand. West follows with the ◊4 and you play dummy's ◊Q. Because the ◊K lies with West, rather than with East, the queen will win the trick.

Again you see how important it was to lead *towards* the ◊Q, the card that you were hoping would win an extra trick.

There is another type of finesse where you lead an honor in the hope of trapping a higher honor:

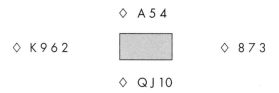

◊ A 5 4

◊ K 9 6 2   ◊ 8 7 3

◊ Q J 10

The ◊Q is accompanied by two neighboring honors, the ◊J and the ◊10. This allows you to lead the ◊Q in an attempt to trap the ◊K. If West plays the ◊K, you will win with the ◊A and your ◊J and ◊10 will be good. Suppose instead that West plays low. You play the ◊4 from dummy and the ◊Q wins the trick. You continue with the ◊J and the situation is the same. Whenever West plays his ◊K, you will end with three diamond tricks.

If East held the king instead, the finesse would fail and you would make only two tricks from the suit.

Provided you have the queen and its two neighbors, the jack and ten, you can trap West's king. Look at this similar position:

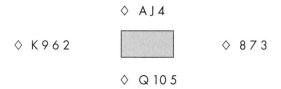

◊ A J 4

◊ K 9 6 2   ◊ 8 7 3

◊ Q 10 5

You lead the ◊Q. If West covers with the ◊K, you will win with the ◊A and make the next two diamond tricks with the ◊J and ◊10.

Do you notice something in common with all these positions? You are leading from the weaker side towards the stronger side. Look back at the last diagram and imagine that you made the mistake of making the first lead from the stronger (North) side. West would then score a trick with the ◊K.

PROBLEM 21

♠ A Q 9 3 2
♡ K 4 3
◇ Q 8 5
♣ 8 7

♡J led

♠ K J 10 8 6
♡ A Q 2
◇ K 6
♣ A Q 6

West	North	East	South
			1♠
pass	2NT	pass	4NT
pass	5◇	pass	6♠
all pass			

You bid adventurously to a small slam in spades (North's Jacoby 2NT showing a strong spade raise) and West leads the ♡J.

You have no losers in spades or hearts. You have one diamond loser, to the ◇A, and two possible losers in clubs. You start with this position:

Losers: ♠ 0 ♡ 0 ◇ 1 ♣ 2 Total: 3

You are certain to lose a diamond trick. How can you give yourself a chance of losing no tricks in clubs?

SOLUTION 21

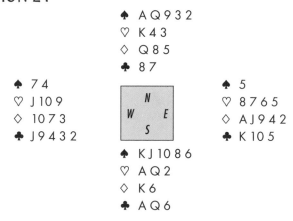

♠ A Q 9 3 2
♡ K 4 3
♢ Q 8 5
♣ 8 7

♠ 7 4
♡ J 10 9
♢ 10 7 3
♣ J 9 4 3 2

♠ 5
♡ 8 7 6 5
♢ A J 9 4 2
♣ K 10 5

♠ K J 10 8 6
♡ A Q 2
♢ K 6
♣ A Q 6

West leads the ♡J against your contract of 6♠. This is the loser position:

Losers: ♠ 0   ♡ 0   ♢ 1   ♣ 2   Total: 3

With a certain loser in diamonds, you must aim to lose no club tricks at all. You will have to take a finesse in the club suit, leading a low club from dummy and finessing the ♣Q (leading from the weak side to the strong side, as usual). If you are lucky and the finesse wins, you will be able to play the ♣A and then ruff your last club in the dummy. How does the play go?

You win the heart lead in either hand and draw trumps with the ♠K and ♠A. You then lead dummy's ♣7, East following with the ♣5. You play the ♣Q from your hand and luck is with you. Because East holds the ♣K, your queen will win the trick. You score the next trick with the ♣A and then lead the ♣6. Dummy has no clubs left, so you can ruff in the dummy. You have lost no club tricks at all and made the small slam.

> **PLAN: I will win the heart lead and draw trumps with the ♠K and ♠A. I will then lead the ♣7, finessing the ♣Q. If I am lucky and the ♣Q wins, I will ruff my last club in dummy.**

POINT TO REMEMBER

To finesse with an ace-queen combination, it is essential to lead from the hand opposite. You lead towards the hand containing the two honors.

PROBLEM 22

♠ J 9 4 2
♡ A 2
◇ 9 7 3
♣ A Q J 7

♡J led

♠ A K Q 10 8 3
♡ K Q
◇ A 6 5
♣ 5 4

West	North	East	South
	1♣	pass	2♠
pass	3♠	pass	4NT
pass	5♡	pass	6♠
all pass			

When partner opens the bidding, you make a jump shift to suggest that a slam may be possible. Partner supports your spades and you then 'ask for aces' by bidding a Blackwood 4NT. Partner shows two aces and you leap to 6♠. How will you play this contract when West leads the ♡J?

You have no losers in spades or hearts. In diamonds you have two losers; in clubs you have one (since dummy's ♣A covers one of your small clubs). This is your loser situation:

Losers: ♠ 0   ♡ 0   ◇ 2   ♣ 1   Total: 3

You must seek a plan to reduce the number of losers from three to one. Can you see a way? Maybe the club finesse will work, but you must still decide how to avoid one of your diamond losers.

POINT TO REMEMBER

For nearly all finesses, you lead from the weaker side of the suit towards the stronger side. Here you will lead from the ♣54 towards the ♣AQJ7.

SOLUTION 22

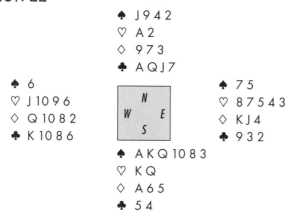

```
                    ♠ J 9 4 2
                    ♡ A 2
                    ◇ 9 7 3
                    ♣ A Q J 7
    ♠ 6                              ♠ 7 5
    ♡ J 10 9 6          N           ♡ 8 7 5 4 3
    ◇ Q 10 8 2      W       E       ◇ K J 4
    ♣ K 10 8 6          S           ♣ 9 3 2
                    ♠ A K Q 10 8 3
                    ♡ K Q
                    ◇ A 6 5
                    ♣ 5 4
```

West leads the ♡J against 6♠. You start with these potential losers:

Losers: ♠ 0   ♡ 0   ◇ 2   ♣ 1   Total: 3

You will need some luck to make this slam. You will need West to hold the ♣K, so that the club finesse will succeed. You can see above that West does hold the ♣K. Hurray! Even so, how can you avoid one of the two potential losers in diamonds?

You must arrange to take the club finesse twice. If you finesse the ♣Q successfully, you will return to your hand and finesse the ♣J. Then you can discard one of your diamond losers on the ♣A. How does the play go?

Although it is not essential, you might as well win the heart lead with dummy's ♡A, since you will need entries to your hand to take the club finesses. Is there any reason not to draw trumps immediately? No, so you do that next.

The time has come to take the club finesse. You lead the ♣4, West follows with the ♣6 and you play dummy's ♣Q. You are dreading the appearance of the ♣K from East but he follows with the ♣2. The finesse has won. You return to your hand with the ♡K and lead the ♣5, West following with the ♣8. You play the ♣J from dummy and this wins the trick. You then play the ♣A and discard one of your diamond losers. You will eventually lose one diamond trick but that is all.

> **PLAN: I will win the heart lead with the ♡A and draw trumps. I will then lead a club, finessing dummy's ♣Q. If the finesse wins, I will return to my hand and lead another club, finessing the ♣J. I can then throw a diamond loser on the ♣A.**

POINT TO REMEMBER

By taking a finesse in one suit, you can sometimes set up a discard for a loser in another suit. Here you performed a 'repeat finesse' in clubs, setting up a discard for a diamond loser.

PROBLEM 23

♠ A 8 6 5
♡ 7 4 3
◇ Q 6 2
♣ 9 8 5

♣Q led

♠ Q J 10 7 4
♡ A K 6
◇ K J 7
♣ A 2

West	North	East	South
			1♠
pass	2♠	pass	4♠
all pass			

North raises to 2♠, showing a minimum hand with spade support. South is then strong enough to bid game in spades. How will you plan the eventual contract of 4♠ when West leads the ♣Q?

You have one possible loser in spades. In hearts you have a slow loser on the third round. You have a further loser in diamonds, since you are missing the ace. There is also a loser in clubs. You start with these potential losers:

Losers: ♠ 1 ♡ 1 ◇ 1 ♣ 1 Total: 4

You need to reduce four losers to three. Which loser do you see a chance of avoiding? How will you play the hand?

SOLUTION 23

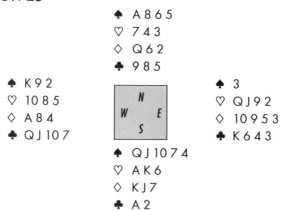

```
            ♠ A 8 6 5
            ♡ 7 4 3
            ◇ Q 6 2
            ♣ 9 8 5
♠ K 9 2                        ♠ 3
♡ 10 8 5          N           ♡ Q J 9 2
◇ A 8 4       W       E       ◇ 10 9 5 3
♣ Q J 10 7        S           ♣ K 6 4 3
            ♠ Q J 10 7 4
            ♡ A K 6
            ◇ K J 7
            ♣ A 2
```

West leads the ♣Q against your spade game and this is the loser position:

Losers: ♠ 1 ♡ 1 ◇ 1 ♣ 1   Total: 4

If you could set up a surplus winner in dummy, you would be able to discard your slow loser in hearts. Unfortunately, there is no possibility of doing this. Nor can you avoid the losers in diamonds and clubs. All will depend on not losing a trump trick to the king. How can this be done?

Until now, the finesses have involved leading towards a high card that you were hoping to score. To give yourself a chance of avoiding a spade loser here, you must use a different type of finesse, and try to trap the ♠K. How does the play go?

After winning with the ♣A, you lead the ♠Q from your hand. West plays the ♠2 and you play low from the dummy, winning the trick. Next you lead the ♠J. If the ♠K appears from West at any stage, you will win with dummy's ♠A. Otherwise you will play low from dummy.

You should lead an honor in a finessing position when your side holds the 'next door neighbors' (the adjacent honors). Usually you will need the card you lead and two neighbors. Here you lead the ♠Q because your side holds the ♠J and ♠10. If the first round goes queen-king-ace (West covering with the king), your jack and ten will score on the next two rounds.

> **PLAN: I will win the club lead and lead the ♠Q intending to finesse. Provided West holds the ♠K, I will lose no spade tricks. After drawing trumps I will play diamonds to establish two tricks there. I will lose one club, one diamond and one heart.**

POINT TO REMEMBER

Lead an honor in a finessing position when your side holds the neighboring honors. Do not lead an honor unless you own the neighboring honors.

PROBLEM 24

♠ Q 5 2
♡ 7 4 2
◇ A 9 4
♣ 10 8 4 2

◇K led

♠ A J 10
♡ A K Q J 8
◇ 7 6 2
♣ A 6

West	North	East	South
			1♡
pass	2♡	pass	4♡
all pass			

West leads the ◇K against your heart game. How will you plan the play?

You have one possible loser in spades and none in hearts. There are two losers in diamonds and one in clubs. This is your loser situation:

Losers: ♠ 1   ♡ 0   ◇ 2   ♣ 1   Total: 4

You must reduce four possible losers to three. Which of the three side suits gives you a chance of reducing the number of losers? How will you play the contract?

SOLUTION 24

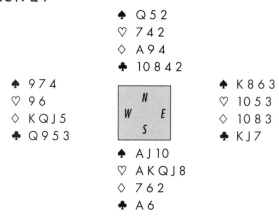

```
              ♠ Q 5 2
              ♡ 7 4 2
              ◊ A 9 4
              ♣ 10 8 4 2
  ♠ 9 7 4                      ♠ K 8 6 3
  ♡ 9 6          N             ♡ 10 5 3
  ◊ K Q J 5    W   E           ◊ 10 8 3
  ♣ Q 9 5 3      S             ♣ K J 7
              ♠ A J 10
              ♡ A K Q J 8
              ◊ 7 6 2
              ♣ A 6
```

You bid to 4♡ and West leads the ◊K. You note this loser position:

Losers: ♠ 1   ♡ 0   ◊ 2   ♣ 1   Total: 4

Even a magician might find it hard to reduce the number of losers in the minor suits. Your only real chance is to avoid the spade loser by taking a finesse in the suit. Because your ♠Q is accompanied by the two neighboring honors (the ♠J and ♠10) you will be able to lead a high card (here the ♠Q) for the finesse. You hope that East holds the ♠K and that you can trap that card. How does the play go?

You win the diamond lead with dummy's ◊A and the first question to ask yourself is: should I draw trumps straight away? What do you think?

If you start to draw trumps at Trick 2, you will never be able to reach dummy again! You would have to lead spades from your hand, allowing the defenders to score a trick with the ♠K, whichever of them holds that card. Since you are in dummy for the last time, you should take the spade finesse immediately. What is more, you must lead the ♠Q. There is nothing that East can do. If he covers the ♠Q with the ♠K, you will win with the ace and later score two more spade tricks with the neighboring honors. If East does not cover, the ♠Q will win the trick and you will still be in dummy to take a second spade finesse, leading to the ♠AJ.

> **PLAN: I will win with the ◊A and lead the ♠Q, hoping to trap the ♠K with East. If East holds the ♠K and does not cover, I will lead a low spade from dummy on the next round, finessing the ♠J. I will eventually lose only two diamonds and one club.**

POINT TO REMEMBER

When you win the first trick in dummy, you may need to use this entry to take a finesse in one of the side suits. This is one of the possible reasons for not drawing trumps straight away.

PROBLEM 25

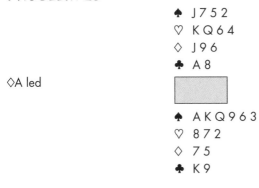

♠ J 7 5 2
♡ K Q 6 4
◊ J 9 6
♣ A 8

◊A led

♠ A K Q 9 6 3
♡ 8 7 2
◊ 7 5
♣ K 9

West	North	East	South
			1♠
pass	3♠	pass	4♠
all pass			

You bid to the spade game and West leads the ◊A. He continues with the ◊K and then leads a third round of diamonds to East's ◊Q, which you ruff. How will you continue the play?

You have no losers in spades, the trump suit. In hearts you have two potential losers. You will make at least one trick with dummy's ♡KQ and this will cover one of the three possible heart losers in your hand. You have two diamond losers and no club losers. This is your starting position:

Losers: ♠ 0   ♡ 2   ◊ 2   ♣ 0   Total: 4

The defenders have already claimed their two diamond tricks. You must therefore try to lose only one further trick in the heart suit. How will you play the hand?

SOLUTION 25

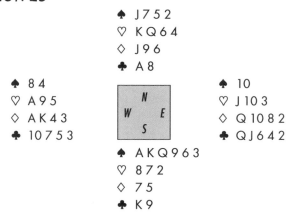

```
                 ♠ J 7 5 2
                 ♡ K Q 6 4
                 ◇ J 9 6
                 ♣ A 8
   ♠ 8 4                            ♠ 10
   ♡ A 9 5          N               ♡ J 10 3
   ◇ A K 4 3     W     E            ◇ Q 10 8 2
   ♣ 10 7 5 3       S               ♣ Q J 6 4 2
                 ♠ A K Q 9 6 3
                 ♡ 8 7 2
                 ◇ 7 5
                 ♣ K 9
```

West leads the ◇A against your spade game. He continues with the ◇K and the ◇3, East playing the ◇Q on the third round. You ruff in your hand and see that this is the loser position:

Losers: ♠ 0 ♡ 2 ◇ 2 ♣ 0 Total: 4

You have already lost two diamond tricks, so you will need to restrict the heart losers to one. How can you do this?

You will have to lead towards dummy's ♡KQ64, hoping that West holds the ♡A. By leading (twice) from the weak side of the heart suit towards the strong side, you hope to escape for just one heart loser. How does the play go?

After ruffing the third round of diamonds, you draw trumps with the ♠A and ♠K. You then lead the ♡2 towards dummy. West follows with the ♡5 and you play dummy's ♡Q. You are in luck. Because West (rather than East) holds the ♡A, dummy's ♡Q will win the trick. What will you do next?

You need to repeat the heart finesse. You return to your hand with the ♣K and lead the ♡7. There is nothing that West can do. Whether he rises with the ♡A or plays low for a second time, you will score a second heart trick with dummy's ♡K. You will lose only one heart trick and make the contract.

> **PLAN: I will ruff the third diamond and draw trumps, then lead a low heart towards dummy, playing the ♡Q unless West rises with the ♡A. If the ♡Q wins, I will return to hand and lead towards the ♡K. If West holds the ♡A, I will make the contract.**

POINT TO REMEMBER _____

When finessing, you lead from the weak side of the suit towards the strong side. Here you lead hearts from the weak (South) side towards the strong (North) side.

PROBLEM 26

♠ A 7 5 2
♡ K J 4
◇ 8 5 2
♣ A 10 8

◇Q led

♠ K Q J 6 3
♡ A 5 2
◇ 9 6 4
♣ K 5

West	North	East	South
	1♣	pass	1♠
pass	2♠	pass	4♠
all pass			

West leads the ◇Q against your spade game. When this card wins the trick, he continues with a low diamond to East's ◇K. East plays the ◇A next, giving the defenders the first three tricks. How will you play the contract when East then switches to the ♠9?

This was your initial loser situation:

Losers: ♠ 0   ♡ 1   ◇ 3   ♣ 0   Total: 4

The defenders have already taken their three diamond tricks, so you cannot afford to lose a heart trick. What plan will you make? How will you play the hand?

SOLUTION 26

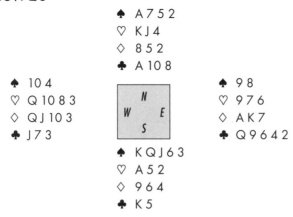

```
              ♠ A 7 5 2
              ♡ K J 4
              ◇ 8 5 2
              ♣ A 10 8
♠ 10 4                        ♠ 9 8
♡ Q 10 8 3       N            ♡ 9 7 6
◇ Q J 10 3    W     E         ◇ A K 7
♣ J 7 3          S            ♣ Q 9 6 4 2
              ♠ K Q J 6 3
              ♡ A 5 2
              ◇ 9 6 4
              ♣ K 5
```

West leads the ◇Q against 4♠ and this is the loser position:

Losers: ♠ 0   ♡ 1   ◇ 3   ♣ 0   Total: 4

The defenders take three diamond tricks and East then switches to the ♣9. How can you avoid losing a trick in hearts? You cannot ruff a heart in dummy. Nor does dummy have any surplus winner on which you can discard a heart. You will have to use the third main method for reducing the number of losers — finessing. You are missing the ♡Q but by finessing dummy's ♡J, you may be able to score all three heart tricks. How does the play go?

The defenders take three diamond tricks and you win East's ♣9 with the ♣K. You then play the ♠Q, drawing the defenders' trumps. The time has come to take a heart finesse. You play the ♡A on the first round, just in case East has a singleton ♡Q. You then lead the ♡2 towards dummy's ♡KJ. (As usual, you are leading from the weak side of the suit towards the strong side.) West follows with the ♡8 and you play the ♡J from dummy. Good news arrives! East does not hold the ♡Q and dummy's ♡J wins the trick. You will make the remaining tricks and score up your game.

> **PLAN: I will win the trump switch and draw trumps. I will then play the ♡A and lead a low heart towards dummy, finessing the ♡J. I will make the game when West holds the ♡Q.**

POINT TO REMEMBER

With this heart combination the finesse comes on the second round of the suit. You start by playing the ♡A and then lead a low card from the weak side (South) towards the ♡KJ. It would be a big mistake to play the ♡K on the first round. You would not then be able to take a finesse in the suit.

PROBLEM 27

<pre>
            ♠ 10 8 5 3
            ♡ A J 7
            ◇ 9 7 6
            ♣ Q 7 6
♠A led
            ┌─────────┐
            │   │
            └─────────┘
            ♠ 7 6
            ♡ K Q 8 5 2
            ◇ A K Q
            ♣ A 8 4
</pre>

West	North	East	South
			1♡
pass	2♡	pass	4♡
all pass			

North correctly shows his heart support, rather than bidding spades, and South is then strong enough to bid game. How will you plan the contract of 4♡ when West leads the ♠A, continuing with the ♠K and another spade to East's ♠J?

You have lost two spade tricks and have no losers in hearts, the trump suit. Your diamonds are solid and there are two possible losers in clubs. These are the tricks that you might lose:

Losers: ♠ 2 ♡ 0 ◇ 0 ♣ 2 Total: 4

How can you give yourself a chance of losing one club trick instead of two? There is no chance of ruffing a club in dummy, nor does dummy have any surplus winners that could be used for a discard. You will have to rely on the third main method of saving a loser — finessing.

How will you play the contract?

SOLUTION 27

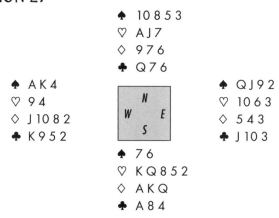

```
                    ♠  10 8 5 3
                    ♡  A J 7
                    ◇  9 7 6
                    ♣  Q 7 6
  ♠ A K 4                                ♠ Q J 9 2
  ♡ 9 4              N                    ♡ 10 6 3
  ◇ J 10 8 2    W         E              ◇ 5 4 3
  ♣ K 9 5 2          S                    ♣ J 10 3
                    ♠  7 6
                    ♡  K Q 8 5 2
                    ◇  A K Q
                    ♣  A 8 4
```

West leads the ace, king and another spade against your heart game. You have these possible losers:

Losers: ♠ 2   ♡ 0   ◇ 0   ♣ 2   Total: 4

You have lost two spade tricks already, so you must look for some play in clubs that will give you a chance of losing only one club trick. The ♣A is certain to score a trick. You must lead *towards* the ♣Q, the card that you are hoping will give you an extra trick. If you are lucky and West holds the ♣K, you will make the contract. How does the play go?

You ruff the third round of spades and draw trumps in three rounds. You then play the ♣A and lead the ♣4 from your hand towards dummy. West follows with the ♣5 and you play dummy's ♣Q. It wins the trick because it is West rather than East who holds the ♣K. You will lose only one club trick and the game is yours.

Suppose West decides to play the ♣K on the second round. You will still lose only one club trick, making tricks with the ♣A and ♣Q.

> **PLAN: I will ruff the third round of spades and draw trumps. I will then lead the ♣A and lead towards the ♣Q. If West holds the ♣K, I will make the contract.**

POINT TO REMEMBER _____

The only real chance of making a trick with the ♣Q is to lead a low card towards it, hoping that West holds the ♣K. Suppose you mistakenly led the ♣Q from dummy instead. You would never make more than one club trick. Either East would cover with the ♣K, forcing your ♣A, or the ♣Q would lose to West's ♣K.

PROBLEM 28

♠ A 10 6 5
♡ A 3
♢ A J 10
♣ 10 6 4 2

♡9 led

[ ]

♠ 2
♡ K Q J 10 7 6 2
♢ 7 6 3
♣ J 7

West	North	East	South
			3♡
pass	4♡	all pass	

You open with a preemptive 3♡ bid, showing a good seven-card heart suit but not enough points to open 1♡. North raises you to 4♡ and West leads the nine of trumps. How will you plan the contract?

You have no losers in spades or hearts. In diamonds you have two potential losers, since dummy's ace covers one of your three low cards. In clubs you have two quick losers and no real chance of avoiding them.

This is your initial loser count:

Losers: ♠ 0   ♡ 0   ♢ 2   ♣ 2   Total: 4

You must aim to reduce your two potential diamond losers to just one loser. How will you play the hand?

SOLUTION 28

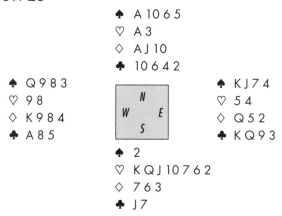

♠ A 10 6 5
♡ A 3
◇ A J 10
♣ 10 6 4 2

♠ Q 9 8 3
♡ 9 8
◇ K 9 8 4
♣ A 8 5

♠ K J 7 4
♡ 5 4
◇ Q 5 2
♣ K Q 9 3

♠ 2
♡ K Q J 10 7 6 2
◇ 7 6 3
♣ J 7

West leads the ♡9 against your game in hearts. You start with these losers:

Losers: ♠ 0   ♡ 0   ◇ 2   ♣ 2   Total: 4

You have no real chance of avoiding the club losers and must aim to lose just one diamond trick. The only prospect of doing this is by taking two finesses in the diamond suit. You will play low to the ◇J on the first round. If this loses, as it probably will, you will win East's return and finesse the ◇10. How does the play go?

You win the trump lead with dummy's ace and play a second round of trumps to your king, both defenders following. With the trumps drawn, you lead the ◇3. As usual with a finesse, you are leading towards the honors that you hope will score an extra trick for you. West follows with the ◇4 and you play dummy's ◇J. East wins the trick with the ◇Q and your first finesse has failed.

East takes the next trick with the ♣K and plays a second round of clubs to West's ♣A. You ruff the third round of clubs and now lead the ◇6 towards dummy's remaining ◇A10. West follows with the ◇8 and you play dummy's ◇10. That's better! The second finesse wins because it is West who holds the other missing diamond honor, the ◇K. You have avoided one of your diamond losers and will now make the contract. You will score seven heart tricks, two aces and an extra diamond trick (the ◇10).

> **PLAN: I will draw trumps and take two finesses in diamonds. If the first finesse (leading to the ◇J) fails, I will finesse the ◇10 on the next round. Unless East holds both the ◇K and the ◇Q, I will lose only one diamond trick.**

POINT TO REMEMBER

When you are missing two honors in a suit, you can take a 'double finesse' — you take two finesses in the same suit, one after the other.

PROBLEM 29

♠ K J 9 2
♡ 9 7 4
◇ A Q 5 2
♣ 8 7

♡Q led

```
┌─────────┐
│         │
└─────────┘
```

♠ A Q 10 8 6 5 3
♡ 8 6
◇ 7 6
♣ A Q

West	North	East	South
			1♠
pass	3♠	pass	4♠
all pass			

West leads the ♡Q, continuing with the ♡J and a third heart to East's ♡K. What is your plan for the contract?

You have no spade loser and two heart losers (already conceded). You have one diamond loser (dummy's ◇A covers one of your low cards) and one further loser in clubs. You start with this position:

Losers: ♠ 0 ♡ 2 ◇ 1 ♣ 1 Total: 4

You ruff the third round of hearts and can afford to lose only one further trick in the minor suits (clubs and diamonds). How will you play the contract?

SOLUTION 29

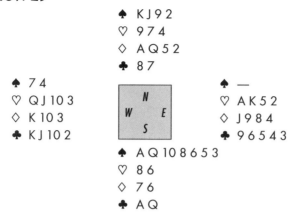

```
                          ♠ K J 9 2
                          ♡ 9 7 4
                          ◇ A Q 5 2
                          ♣ 8 7
     ♠ 7 4                                    ♠ —
     ♡ Q J 10 3          ┌──────────┐         ♡ A K 5 2
     ◇ K 10 3            │    N     │         ◇ J 9 8 4
     ♣ K J 10 2          │ W     E  │         ♣ 9 6 5 4 3
                         │    S     │
                         └──────────┘
                          ♠ A Q 10 8 6 5 3
                          ♡ 8 6
                          ◇ 7 6
                          ♣ A Q
```

West leads the ♡Q against your spade game and continues with ♡J and another heart, East playing the ♡K. This is the loser position:

Losers: ♠ 0 ♡ 2 ◇ 1 ♣ 1 Total: 4

You can afford only one minor-suit loser. Both diamonds and clubs offer you the chance of a 'finesse'. What does this mean? It means that you can lead towards the AQ combination in either suit and play the queen. If you are lucky and the missing king lies with the defender who plays before the hand containing the AQ, the queen will win. One of your potential losers will be avoided.

Here you have two AQ combinations and will take two finesses. If at least one of them succeeds, you will make the game. How does the play go?

You ruff the third heart and play the ♠A and ♠K, drawing the defenders' trumps. You then lead the ♣7 from dummy. East follows low and you play the ♣Q from your hand. This time you're unlucky and West wins with the ♣K.

You win West's ♣J return with the ♣A and must now take your second finesse. You lead the ◇6, West playing the ◇3, and play dummy's ◇Q. Yes, it wins! This time you are lucky and it is the defender playing before the hand with the AQ who holds the missing king. The game is yours.

> **PLAN: I will ruff the third heart, draw trumps and finesse the ♣Q. Whether or not the finesse wins, I will then finesse the ◇Q. If either finesse wins, I will make the contract.**

POINT TO REMEMBER

To finesse with an ace-queen combination, it is essential to lead a low card from the hand opposite. You lead towards the hand containing the two honors.

PROBLEM 30

♠ A Q 10 5
♡ A 5
◇ A K 3
♣ A 6 4 2

♣K led

♠ 6 3 2
♡ K Q J 9 7 6 3
◇ 7 5
♣ 7

West	North	East	South
			3♡
pass	6♡	all pass	

You open with a preemptive 3♡ and North keeps the bidding simple, raising directly to 6♡. What plan will you make when West leads the ♣K?

You start by counting your possible losers. You have two in spades and none in hearts. There are no losers in diamonds or clubs, because dummy's honors cover your losers in those suits.

This is your loser situation:

Losers: ♠ 2 ♡ 0 ◇ 0 ♣ 0 Total: 2

You must do what you can to avoid two spade losers. It seems that you may have to rely on finessing. How will you play the hand?

SOLUTION 30

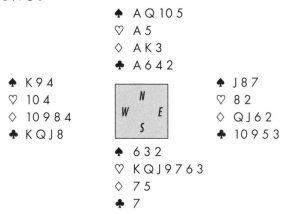

```
              ♠ A Q 10 5
              ♡ A 5
              ◇ A K 3
              ♣ A 6 4 2
♠ K 9 4                        ♠ J 8 7
♡ 10 4          N              ♡ 8 2
◇ 10 9 8 4   W     E           ◇ Q J 6 2
♣ K Q J 8       S              ♣ 10 9 5 3
              ♠ 6 3 2
              ♡ K Q J 9 7 6 3
              ◇ 7 5
              ♣ 7
```

West leads the ♣K against 6♡. You face these potential losers:

Losers: ♠ 2   ♡ 0   ◇ 0   ♣ 0   Total: 2

You win the club lead with dummy's ♣A and draw trumps in two rounds. There is no chance of ruffing or discarding a spade loser, so you will have to rely on finessing. You lead the ♠2 from your hand and West follows with the ♠4. Which card will you play from dummy's ♠AQ10?

Your intention is to take a double finesse in the suit, finessing both the ♠10 and the ♠Q. It is good technique to finesse the lower card (the ♠10) first. You would then lose no spade tricks at all if West held the ♠K and the ♠J. Here, the ♠10 loses to East's jack and you ruff East's club return. You lead another spade from your hand, West following low, and finesse the ♠Q. The second finesse wins and you have reduced the number of spade losers from two to one. Twelve tricks and the slam are yours.

> **PLAN: I will win the club lead and draw trumps. I will take a double finesse in spades (finessing the ♠10 and later finessing the ♠Q). I will make the contract when West holds at least one of the ♠K and ♠J.**

POINT TO REMEMBER

When you take a double finesse (with a combination such as AQ10) you should finesse the **lower card** first. You can then make two extra tricks when both the king and the jack lie with the defender playing before the AQ10.

5

ESTABLISHING A SUIT

In this chapter we will look at various ways of 'establishing a suit' in a trump contract. What does that mean? It means that you play one of your suits until the remaining cards are all winners.

For example, if dummy holds the ♡KQJ opposite your ♡862 you can establish the heart suit (or 'set up' the heart suit) by playing hearts until the defenders take their ace. You will then create two heart winners.

In this chapter we will be looking at establishing suits in a trump contract. Suppose, for example, that dummy holds ◊AK873 and you hold ◊64. When the defenders' cards in the suit break 3-3, you can 'establish the diamonds' by playing the ◊A, the ◊K and then ruffing a diamond in your hand. The defenders will have no diamonds left and dummy's ◊8 and ◊7 will be established as winners.

PROBLEM 31

```
              ♠ K 5 2
              ♡ Q J
              ◊ A K 8 7 3
              ♣ 8 7 2
♣K led        ┌──────────┐
              │          │
              └──────────┘
              ♠ A Q J 10 7 6
              ♡ 8 6
              ◊ 6 4
              ♣ A 9 6
```

West	North	East	South
	1◊	pass	1♠
pass	2♠	pass	4♠
all pass			

West leads the ♣K against your spade game. What is your plan?

You have no spade losers and two quick heart losers. You have no diamond losers, since your two cards are covered by the ◊AK in dummy. In clubs you have two losers. You start with this position:

Losers: ♠0 ♡2 ◊0 ♣2 Total: 4

How will you play the contract?

SOLUTION 31

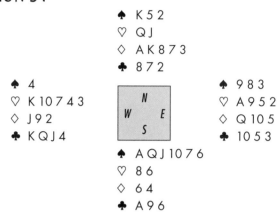

```
                    ♠ K 5 2
                    ♡ Q J
                    ◇ A K 8 7 3
                    ♣ 8 7 2
♠ 4                                      ♠ 9 8 3
♡ K 10 7 4 3        N                    ♡ A 9 5 2
◇ J 9 2          W     E                 ◇ Q 10 5
♣ K Q J 4           S                    ♣ 10 5 3
                    ♠ A Q J 10 7 6
                    ♡ 8 6
                    ◇ 6 4
                    ♣ A 9 6
```

West leads the ♣K against your spade game and this is the loser position:

Losers: ♠ 0   ♡ 2   ◇ 0   ♣ 2   Total: 4

The only possible way to avoid losing four tricks is to establish dummy's diamond suit. When the defenders' diamonds break 3-3, you can play dummy's two top diamonds and then ruff a diamond in your hand. The last two diamonds will be winners and you can discard two of your four losers. How will the play go?

You win the club lead with the ♣A. How you play the trump suit will determine whether or not you make the contract. What is your plan?

Even if diamonds do break 3-3, you will need the ♠K as an entry to reach the two established cards in the suit. After winning the club lead, you should therefore play the ♠A and ♠Q. Here, West shows out on the second round. You cannot afford to draw East's last trump now because you will need the ♠K later as an entry.

You cross to the ◇A. You win a second diamond trick with the ◇K and then lead a third round of diamonds, ruffing with the ♠10 in your hand. Both defenders follow suit, yes! They now have no diamonds left and the ◇8 and ◇7 are established as winners. You return to dummy with the ♠K, drawing East's last trump, and play the two diamond winners, throwing two losers. You have made an overtrick.

> **PLAN: I will win the club lead and play the ♠A and ♠Q. I will then play dummy's top diamonds and ruff a diamond in my hand, hoping for a 3-3 break. If that is the case, I can return to dummy with the ♠K and discard two losers on the ◇8 and ◇7.**

POINT TO REMEMBER

When you are setting up a suit in the dummy, you sometimes have to use an entry in the trump suit to reach the established cards. This may mean that you cannot draw all the trumps before establishing the side suit.

PROBLEM 32

```
        ♠  A 6
        ♡  A 8 7 5
        ◇  A 10
        ♣  A K 9 7 4
♡Q led
        ┌─────────┐
        │         │
        └─────────┘
        ♠  K Q J 10 9 5 3
        ♡  3 2
        ◇  J 7
        ♣  6 2
```

West	North	East	South
			3♠
pass	6♠	all pass	

You open 3♠, showing a weak hand with a seven-card spade suit of good quality. Your partner can see the potential for plenty of tricks and jumps straight to 6♠.

How will you play this contract when West leads the ♡Q?

You have no losers in spades and one in hearts. In diamonds you have one loser. In clubs you have none, because your two cards are covered by dummy's ♣A and ♣K.

You start with two possible losers:

Losers: ♠ 0   ♡ 1   ◇ 1   ♣ 0   Total: 2

No finesses or ruffs will be possible in hearts or diamonds. You need to establish dummy's clubs in order to discard at least one of your losers. As we saw on the first problem, this will be easy if the defenders' clubs break 3-3. Is there any chance when clubs break 4-2?

SOLUTION 32

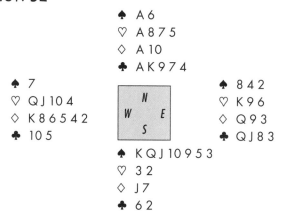

♠ A 6
♥ A 8 7 5
♦ A 10
♣ A K 9 7 4

♠ 7
♥ Q J 10 4
♦ K 8 6 5 4 2
♣ 10 5

♠ 8 4 2
♥ K 9 6
♦ Q 9 3
♣ Q J 8 3

♠ K Q J 10 9 5 3
♥ 3 2
♦ J 7
♣ 6 2

West leads the ♥Q and you start with these potential losers:

Losers: ♠ 0   ♥ 1   ♦ 1   ♣ 0   **Total: 2**

To avoid at least one of these losers, you will need to establish dummy's club suit. By playing the ♣A and ♣K and ruffing a club in declarer's hand, you can set up two club winners if the defenders' cards break 3-3. If instead the defenders' clubs break 4-2, you will need to take a second ruff to exhaust the defenders' cards in the suit. This will establish one good club (the ♣9) in dummy and you will then be able to discard one of your losers. How does the play go?

You win the heart lead with dummy's ace. To enjoy a long card in clubs against a 4-2 break, you will now need two further entries to dummy outside the club suit. One of these is the ♠A, so you cannot afford to draw trumps yet.

You play the ♣A and ♣K immediately and ruff a club with the ♠9, to prevent an overruff. It's just as well you did ruff high, because West is out of clubs. If you had carelessly ruffed with the ♠3 or ♠5, West would have overruffed with the ♠7.

You return to dummy with the ♠A and ruff another club with the ♠10. You then draw the outstanding trumps with the ♠K and ♠Q. Finally, you return to dummy with the ♦A and play the good ♣9, discarding a heart (or a diamond). You will lose one trick eventually but the slam is yours.

> **PLAN: I will win the heart lead and play the ♣A and ♣K. I will then ruff a club with the ♠9. If clubs break 4-2, I will cross to dummy with the ♠A and ruff another club. I can then draw trumps, cross to the ♦A and discard a loser on the long club.**

POINT TO REMEMBER

When you are establishing a suit by ruffing in your hand, the number of ruffs you need will depend on how the defenders' cards break.

PROBLEM 33

♠ K J 2
♡ 8 5
♢ Q 8 7 6 4
♣ 7 4 3

♡Q led

♠ A Q 9 6 5 3
♡ A 4
♢ K 3
♣ A 6 2

West	North	East	South
			1♠
pass	2♠	pass	4♠
all pass			

West leads the ♡Q against your spade game. What plan will you make for the contract?

You start with no losers in spades and one in hearts. In diamonds you have one loser, to the ace, and in clubs there are two losers. This is the starting position:

Losers: ♠0 ♡1 ♢1 ♣2 Total: 4

You cannot hope to avoid the two red-suit losers. Your aim must be to discard one or both club losers on dummy's diamond suit.

How will the defenders' diamonds have to break to allow you to establish dummy's suit. How will you play the hand?

POINT TO REMEMBER

When you plan the entries that you will need, remember that the defenders may make life difficult for you. On this deal, for example, suppose you lead the ♢K at some stage and East has the ♢A. He will probably 'hold up' the ace on the first round, following with a low card. This will prevent you from using dummy's ♢Q as an entry on the second round.

SOLUTION 33

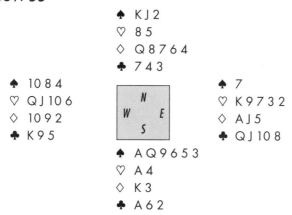

```
                      ♠ K J 2
                      ♡ 8 5
                      ◇ Q 8 7 6 4
                      ♣ 7 4 3
    ♠ 10 8 4                          ♠ 7
    ♡ Q J 10 6          N             ♡ K 9 7 3 2
    ◇ 10 9 2        W       E         ◇ A J 5
    ♣ K 9 5             S             ♣ Q J 10 8
                      ♠ A Q 9 6 5 3
                      ♡ A 4
                      ◇ K 3
                      ♣ A 6 2
```

West leads the ♡Q against your spade game and this is the loser position:

Losers: ♠ 0   ♡ 1   ◇ 1   ♣ 2   Total: 4

You need to establish dummy's diamonds, so that you can discard one or both of your club losers. Even if the defenders' diamonds break 3-3, as you would like, you must make sure that you have enough dummy entries to carry out your plan.

    You win the heart lead and see that you may have to use dummy's ♠K and ♠J as entries, to set up the diamond suit and enjoy the established winners. You can draw one round of trumps with the ♠A but must then turn to the diamond suit. When you lead the ◇K, East will probably play low and let it win. This is good defense, stopping you from crossing to dummy with the ◇Q on the second round.

    Now you lead the ◇3, playing dummy's ◇Q, and East wins with the ◇A. You win his club switch with the ♣A and are now very glad that you retained dummy's ♠K and ♠J as entries! You cross to the ♠J, East showing out, and lead the ◇6 from dummy. When you ruff with the ♠Q, West follows suit. The diamonds have broken 3-3. Hurray! You return to dummy with the ♠K and discard both your club losers on the ◇8 and ◇7. You have made an overtrick.

> **PLAN: I will win with the ♡A, play the ♠A and lead the ◇K. When the defenders' diamonds break 3-3, I can use the ♠K and ♠J as entries to establish the diamonds, even if the defenders hold up the ◇A. I can then discard both my club losers.**

PROBLEM 34

```
                    ♠ 6 4 3
                    ♡ A 8 5
                    ◇ J 8 6
                    ♣ 10 8 5 4
```

♡Q led

```
                    ♠ A K Q J 9 7
                    ♡ K 4 3
                    ◇ A
                    ♣ A K 2
```

West	North	East	South
			2♣
pass	2◇	pass	2♠
pass	3♠	pass	4NT
pass	5◇	pass	6♠
all pass			

South's 2♠ rebid is forcing to game. North's 3♠ shows a spade fit and a useful card or two. South heads for a small slam in spades and West leads the ♡Q.

What plan will you make, as declarer?

You have no spade losers and one loser in hearts. The singleton ace means that you have no loser in diamonds. In clubs you have one loser. This is the loser situation:

Losers: ♠ 0   ♡ 1   ◇ 0   ♣ 1   **Total: 2**

You must somehow reduce the number of losers from two to one. How will you play the hand?

SOLUTION 34

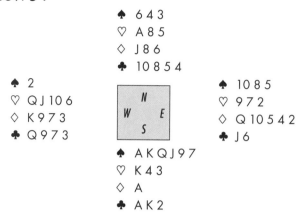

```
                    ♠ 6 4 3
                    ♡ A 8 5
                    ◇ J 8 6
                    ♣ 10 8 5 4
    ♠ 2                           ♠ 10 8 5
    ♡ Q J 10 6          N         ♡ 9 7 2
    ◇ K 9 7 3       W       E     ◇ Q 10 5 4 2
    ♣ Q 9 7 3           S         ♣ J 6
                    ♠ A K Q J 9 7
                    ♡ K 4 3
                    ◇ A
                    ♣ A K 2
```

West leads the ♡Q against 6♠ and you face these potential losers:

Losers: ♠ 0   ♡ 1   ◇ 0   ♣ 1   Total: 2

Easily the best chance of making the contract is to establish an extra winner in clubs. You can then use the surplus winner to discard your heart loser.

One chance is that clubs will break 3-3. When you play the ♣A, the ♣K and then the ♣2, this will exhaust the defenders' clubs. Dummy's last club will be a winner. In fact, there is a substantial second chance of scoring an extra club trick. When East holds a doubleton queen or jack, your second high club will drop his honor. You can then lead towards the ♣10 on the third round, setting it up as an extra winner. How does the play go?

You win the heart lead with the ♡K, to preserve dummy's ♡A as an entry. You draw trumps in three rounds. Next, you play the ♣A and ♣K, noting with great pleasure that the ♣J falls from East. When you lead the ♣2 towards dummy's ♣10, there is nothing West can do. If he plays the ♣Q, dummy's ♣10 will be good and you can reach it with the ♡A. If instead West plays the ♣9, you will cover with dummy's ♣10. This will guarantee an extra club trick, whichever defender happens to hold the ♣Q.

Let's say that West does play his ♣Q and then leads the ♡J. You win with dummy's ♡A and play the established ♣10, throwing your heart loser.

> **PLAN: I will win with the ♡K, draw trumps and play ace, king and another club. When clubs break 3-3 or East holds a doubleton ♣Q or ♣J, I will establish a club winner in the dummy. I will cross to the ♡A and discard my heart loser.**

POINT TO REMEMBER

Sometimes there are several chances of establishing a suit.

PROBLEM 35

♠ 7 6 3
♡ A 5
♢ 1 0 8 7 6 4 2
♣ K 8

♣Q led

♠ A 9 4
♡ K Q J 10 9 4
♢ A K
♣ A 2

West	North	East	South
			2♣
pass	2♢	pass	2♡
pass	3♢	pass	3♡
pass	6♡	all pass	

South's 2♡ rebid is forcing to game, even if North holds nothing of value. North is too strong to bid just 4♡ over 3♡. Taking a favorable view of his hand, he leaps all the way to 6♡.

What is your plan for the small slam when West leads the ♣Q?

You have two possible losers in spades and no further losers in the other suits. This is your starting position:

Losers: ♠ 2 ♡ 0 ♢ 0 ♣ 0 Total: 2

Do you see any possibility of avoiding one or both of your spade losers? How will you play the hand?

SOLUTION 35

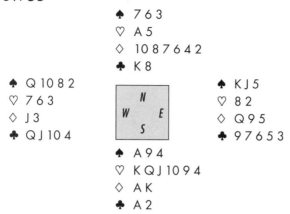

♠ 7 6 3
♡ A 5
◇ 10 8 7 6 4 2
♣ K 8

♠ Q 10 8 2
♡ 7 6 3
◇ J 3
♣ Q J 10 4

♠ K J 5
♡ 8 2
◇ Q 9 5
♣ 9 7 6 5 3

♠ A 9 4
♡ K Q J 10 9 4
◇ A K
♣ A 2

West leads the ♣Q against your heart slam and this is the loser position:

Losers: ♠ 2   ♡ 0   ◇ 0   ♣ 0   Total: 2

There is no possibility of ruffing a spade in dummy or taking a spade finesse. The only hope is to establish dummy's diamonds and to discard one or both spade losers on the surplus diamond winners in dummy. How will the play go?

Since you will need an entry to dummy to reach the established diamonds, you should win the club lead in your hand with the ♣A. You cannot afford to draw all the trumps straight away because you will have to use dummy's ♡A as an entry. Your next move must be to play the ◇A and ◇K. If one of these cards is ruffed by a defender, you will go down. Yes, but in that case (with diamonds breaking 4-1) you could never have made the contract.

When the cards lie as in the diagram, both defenders will follow to the two diamonds. You cross to dummy with the ♡A, using your entry in the trump suit to good effect, and ruff a diamond with the ♡9. You have established dummy's diamond suit. You draw the outstanding trumps and cross to dummy's other entry, the ♣K, to play two good diamonds. You discard both your spade losers and make an overtrick!

> **PLAN: I will win with the ♣A and play the ◇A and ◇K. When both defenders follow suit, I cross to the ♡A and ruff a diamond with the ♡9. I can then draw trumps and return to dummy with the ♣K to discard my spade losers on the established diamonds.**

POINT TO REMEMBER _____

On deals like these, you must use the trump entry (♡A) to dummy before the side-suit entry (♣K). This will allow you to draw all the trumps before returning to dummy to take your discards.

PROBLEM 36

♠ J 10 2
♡ 9 7 6 5 3
♢ 9 8 3
♣ J 9

◊Q led

♠ A K Q 6 5 3
♡ 8 4
♢ A K 2
♣ A 3

West	North	East	South
			2♣
pass	2◊	pass	2♠
pass	4♠	all pass	

West leads the ◊Q against your spade game. How will you plan the play?

You have no losers in spades and two in hearts. In diamonds there is one loser on the third round and you also have a club loser. You have a total of four losers:

Losers: ♠ 0   ♡ 2   ◊ 1   ♣ 1   Total: 4

The situation looks grim and you sit there for a moment, wishing you had somehow ended in 3NT. It's too late for that! You must find a way to avoid one of your losers. If you need a lucky break somewhere, perhaps you will be granted it.

SOLUTION 36

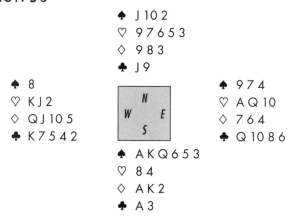

```
              ♠ J 10 2
              ♡ 9 7 6 5 3
              ◇ 9 8 3
              ♣ J 9
   ♠ 8                        ♠ 9 7 4
   ♡ K J 2          N         ♡ A Q 10
   ◇ Q J 10 5    W     E      ◇ 7 6 4
   ♣ K 7 5 4 2       S         ♣ Q 10 8 6
              ♠ A K Q 6 5 3
              ♡ 8 4
              ◇ A K 2
              ♣ A 3
```

You bid to 4♠ and West leads the ◇Q, which you win in your hand. These are your losers:

Losers: ♠ 0   ♡ 2   ◇ 1   ♣ 1   Total: 4

The only chance to avoid one of your minor-suit losers is to establish dummy's heart suit. This may seem a distant prospect but it can be done if hearts break 3-3. You cannot afford to draw a single round of trumps before starting on the hearts, because you will need the ♠J and ♠10 as entries. How does the play go?

After winning the diamond lead with the ace, you lead a heart from your hand. Let's say that East wins with the ♡10 and returns a diamond to your king. You give the defenders another heart trick and they then score a diamond trick. You win the club switch, draw two rounds of trumps with the ♠A and ♠10 and ruff a heart in your hand. Hearts break 3-3! You draw the outstanding trump with the ♠J. Finally, you discard your club loser on one of dummy's good hearts and make your game.

> **PLAN: I win with the ◇A and give up a heart trick. I win the diamond return and give up another heart trick. When I regain the lead, I can draw two rounds of trumps with the ♠A and ♠10 and ruff a heart. This will establish the heart suit if it breaks 3-3. The ♠J will be an entry to the good hearts.**

POINT TO REMEMBER

However weak a suit may be, you can still establish winners there if you can remove all the defenders' cards in the suit.

PROBLEM 37

♠ A J 2
♡ A 10 8
◇ A 9 8 4 3
♣ 9 3

◇K led

♠ K Q 10 7 5 4 3
♡ 7 4 3
◇ 7
♣ J 8

West	North	East	South
			3♠
pass	4♠	all pass	

You open with a preemptive 3♠ and West leads the ◇K against your eventual contract of 4♠. Can you see any chance of making ten tricks?

You have no losers in spades and two in hearts. There are no diamond losers and two quick losers in clubs. This is the initial position:

Losers: ♠ 0 ♡ 2 ◇ 0 ♣ 2 Total: 4

Over to you, then. How will you play the hand?

POINT TO REMEMBER

When you are planning to set up a long suit in the dummy, it is essential to look closely at the entry situation. You may need several entries to take ruffs in the suit to be established. After drawing trumps, you will have to return to dummy to take discards on the surplus winners that you have created. Remember that the trump suit is often a useful source of entries to the dummy.

SOLUTION 37

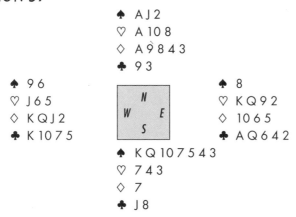

```
              ♠ A J 2
              ♡ A 10 8
              ◇ A 9 8 4 3
              ♣ 9 3
♠ 9 6                          ♠ 8
♡ J 6 5         N              ♡ K Q 9 2
◇ K Q J 2    W     E           ◇ 10 6 5
♣ K 10 7 5      S              ♣ A Q 6 4 2
              ♠ K Q 10 7 5 4 3
              ♡ 7 4 3
              ◇ 7
              ♣ J 8
```

West leads the ◇K against your spade game and this is the loser position:

Losers: ♠ 0   ♡ 2   ◇ 0   ♣ 2   **Total: 4**

The only way to save a heart or club loser is to establish dummy's diamond suit, so that you can take a discard. The defenders' diamonds will have to break 4-3. In that case, by ruffing three diamonds in your hand, you can set up dummy's last diamond as a surplus winner.

You will need four entries to the dummy — three to take diamond ruffs and one to reach the established card in the suit. Your entries will be the three aces and the jack of trumps. Since the ◇A has been removed by the opening lead, you must use this entry immediately, to ruff a diamond in your hand. How will the play go?

After winning with the ◇A, you ruff a diamond in your hand. You cross to the ♠J and ruff another diamond. (Since you have plenty of high trumps, you might as well ruff both these diamonds with a trump honor.) Both defenders follow to the first three rounds of diamonds, so you will now make the contract. You return to dummy with the ♠A, drawing West's last trump, and ruff yet another diamond. Neither defender has any diamonds left and dummy's ◇9 is now good. You return to dummy with the ♡A and lead the established ◇9, discarding a heart (or a club). The game is yours.

> **PLAN: I will win the diamond lead and ruff a diamond immediately, making use of the entry. I will use the ♠J and ♠A as entries to ruff two more diamonds in my hand. When diamonds break 4-3, I will cross to the ♡A to discard a loser on the established diamond.**

PROBLEM 38

♠ 8 5
♡ K 10 3
◇ K 8 3
♣ J 7 6 4 2

♠J led

♠ A K
♡ A Q J 9 8 7
◇ A 7 5
♣ A 8

West	North	East	South
			2♣
pass	2◇	pass	2♡
pass	3♡	pass	6♡
all pass			

North's rebid of 3♡ is stronger than 4♡ would be and shows a useful card or two. South then leaps to a small slam in hearts.

How will you play the contract when West leads the ♠J?

You have no losers in spades or hearts. In diamonds you have one loser and in clubs you have another loser. You start with two losers:

Losers: ♠ 0   ♡ 0   ◇ 1   ♣ 1   **Total: 2**

It seems that you will have to establish dummy's club suit. Can you do this if the defenders' clubs break 4-2? How will you make the best use of dummy's entries?

POINT TO REMEMBER _____

When you are trying to set up a suit where you hold five cards in dummy opposite two in your hand, you will have to take two ruffs to succeed against a 4-2 break. This may require careful attention to your entries.

SOLUTION 38

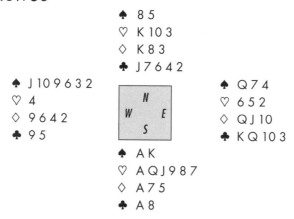

```
              ♠ 8 5
              ♡ K 10 3
              ◇ K 8 3
              ♣ J 7 6 4 2
♠ J 10 9 6 3 2              ♠ Q 7 4
♡ 4            N            ♡ 6 5 2
◇ 9 6 4 2    W   E          ◇ Q J 10
♣ 9 5          S            ♣ K Q 10 3
              ♠ A K
              ♡ A Q J 9 8 7
              ◇ A 7 5
              ♣ A 8
```

West leads the ♠J against 6♡ and this is the loser position:

Losers: ♠ 0   ♡ 0   ◇ 1   ♣ 1   Total: 2

You need to establish dummy's club suit. You will lead the ♣A on the first round (the high card from the shorter side) and then lead the ♣8, giving up a trick in the suit. To establish the clubs when the suit breaks 4-2, you will need to cross to dummy twice to ruff clubs in your hand. Finally, you will need to return to dummy to enjoy the established thirteenth club. You will need a total of three entries to dummy (the ♡10, ♡K and ◇K). How does the play go?

You win the spade lead, play the ♣A and then the ♣8. East wins the trick and switches to the ◇Q. You win with the ◇A, keeping dummy's ◇K as an entry for later. You cross to the ♡10 and ruff a club in your hand, West showing out. Clubs break 4-2, so you will have to ruff another club in your hand. You return to dummy with the ♡K and ruff another club. You then draw East's last trump. Finally you cross to dummy's ◇K and discard your diamond loser on the established ♣7. You have made the slam!

> **PLAN: I will win the spade lead and play the ♣A, followed by the ♣8. I will win the return and cross to dummy's ♡10 to ruff a club in my hand. If the suit breaks 4-2, I will cross to the ♡K to ruff another club. I will then cross to the ◇K to throw a loser on dummy's last club.**

PROBLEM 39

♠ J 6 2
♡ J 8 5
◇ A K Q 7 6
♣ Q 7

♣J led

♠ A K Q 5 4 3
♡ A 4 3
◇ 8 2
♣ A 2

West	North	East	South
	1◇	pass	2♠
pass	3♠	pass	4NT
pass	5◇	pass	5NT
pass	6◇	pass	6♠
all pass			

The spade fit is found and North then shows one ace and one king. How will you play the eventual contract of 6♠ when West leads the ♣J?

You have no losers in spades and two in hearts. In diamonds you have no losers and in clubs you have one. This is your initial loser count:

Losers: ♠ 0   ♡ 2   ◇ 0   ♣ 1   **Total: 3**

You might as well try your luck with dummy's ♣Q on the first trick, but East covers with the ♣K. You win with the ♣A and must now look for the best way to reduce three losers to one. How will you play the hand?

SOLUTION 39

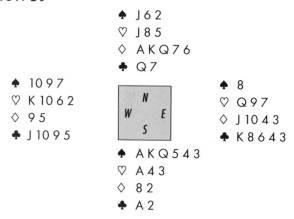

```
              ♠ J 6 2
              ♡ J 8 5
              ◇ A K Q 7 6
              ♣ Q 7
♠ 10 9 7                        ♠ 8
♡ K 10 6 2      N              ♡ Q 9 7
◇ 9 5        W     E           ◇ J 10 4 3
♣ J 10 9 5      S              ♣ K 8 6 4 3
              ♠ A K Q 5 4 3
              ♡ A 4 3
              ◇ 8 2
              ♣ A 2
```

West leads the ♣J against 6♠. You cover with the ♣Q but East produces the ♣K, which you win with the ♣A. You have these potential losers:

Losers: ♠ 0   ♡ 2   ◇ 0   ♣ 1   Total: 3

You must aim to discard at least two of your losers on dummy's diamond suit. After winning the first trick with the ♣A, you play the ♠A and ♠K. East shows out on the second round, so West still has a trump. What next?

If you draw the last trump immediately, you will remove the ♠J entry to dummy. You will have to play the ◇A, ◇K and ◇Q and will need the diamonds to break 3-3 to score more than three diamond tricks. A better idea is to establish the diamonds even when the suit breaks 4-2. You can then use the ♠J as an entry to reach the good diamonds in dummy. After two rounds of trumps you lead a diamond to the ◇A and play the ◇K, both defenders following. In case the diamonds break 4-2, your next move is to lead the ◇6 and ruff in your hand with the ♠Q. (You ruff high to avoid a possible overruff.) West shows out of diamonds on this trick.

Dummy's last two diamonds are the ◇Q and the ◇7. Since East has only one diamond left, this will fall under the ◇Q and dummy's last diamond will then be good. You return to dummy with the ♠J, drawing West's last trump. You then play the ◇Q and the ◇7, discarding two losers.

> **PLAN: After winning the club lead, I will play the ♠A and ♠K. If trumps are 3-1, I cannot afford to draw the last trump. I will play the ◇A and ◇K and ruff a diamond with the ♠Q. I can then cross to the ♠J and throw two losers on the ◇Q7.**

POINT TO REMEMBER

Even when dummy's long suit is headed by the AKQ, a ruff in your hand may protect you against a bad break.

PROBLEM 40

```
                    ♠ K 6 2
                    ♡ 8 5
                    ◇ A 10 7 6 4 3
                    ♣ 7 5
♣Q led          ┌─────────┐
                │         │
                └─────────┘
                    ♠ A 5 3
                    ♡ A K Q J 3 2
                    ◇ 8 2
                    ♣ A K
```

West	North	East	South
	2◇	pass	3♡
pass	4♡	pass	6♡
all pass			

North opened with a weak 2◇ and South bid enthusiastically to a slam in hearts. Whatever you think of the bidding, there is nothing much wrong with the final contract of 6♡.

How will you plan the play of the slam when West leads the ♣Q?

You have one potential loser in spades and none in hearts, the trump suit. There is one diamond loser and no club loser. These are your possible losers:

Losers: ♠ 1   ♡ 0   ◇ 1   ♣ 0   Total: 2

The diamond loser is a near certainty, so you will have to make plans for your spade loser. Perhaps you can establish dummy's diamonds. What do you think?

SOLUTION 40

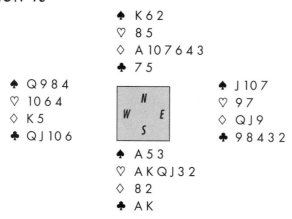

```
              ♠ K 6 2
              ♡ 8 5
              ◇ A 10 7 6 4 3
              ♣ 7 5
♠ Q 9 8 4                        ♠ J 10 7
♡ 10 6 4          N             ♡ 9 7
◇ K 5        W         E        ◇ Q J 9
♣ Q J 10 6        S             ♣ 9 8 4 3 2
              ♠ A 5 3
              ♡ A K Q J 3 2
              ◇ 8 2
              ♣ A K
```

West leads the ♣Q against 6♡. These are the possible losers:

Losers: ♠ 1   ♡ 0   ◇ 1   ♣ 0   Total: 2

How can you avoid the spade loser? You must establish dummy's diamonds and then return to dummy to take a spade discard on one of the good diamonds. How can this be done?

You win the club lead and draw trumps in three rounds. What will happen if you now play a diamond to the ace? You will go down! The defenders will win the second round and you will have to use the ♠K as an entry to establish the diamonds with a ruff; there will be no entry to dummy to score an extra diamond trick.

Instead you must make a clever move — you must duck the first round of diamonds (allowing the defenders to win the trick). This will leave dummy's ◇A as an entry on the second round. You lead the ◇2 and play the ◇3 (or any other low diamond) from dummy. East wins and returns the ♠J. Because you will need the ♠K as an entry to dummy later, you win with the ♠A.

You cross to the ◇A, both defenders following, and ruff a diamond in your hand. Dummy's diamonds are then established; neither defender has any diamonds left. You return to dummy with the ♠K and lead the ◇10, discarding your spade loser. You have made the slam.

> **PLAN: I will win the club lead, draw trumps and duck a round of diamonds. I will win the club return, cross to the ◇A and set up the diamonds with a ruff (if they break 3-2). I will then cross to the ♠K and discard the ♠5 on a good diamond.**

POINT TO REMEMBER

When you are setting up a suit in dummy, you sometimes have to duck the first round, using dummy's high card in the suit as a second-round entry.

PART 2

NOTRUMP CONTRACTS

6

COUNTING WINNERS IN A NOTRUMP CONTRACT

The time has come for us to look at notrump contracts. To plan a notrump contract, you start by counting your 'top tricks'. What does that mean? It means tricks that you could take immediately if you wanted to. Any suit headed by the ace will have at least one top trick. If you also hold the king of that suit, in your own hand or the dummy, you will have at least two top tricks in the suit. In a suit where the defenders hold the ace, you will not have any top tricks at all.

The first step in making a plan is to take each suit in turn and count the tricks that are immediately available. We will start by looking at some suit combinations and counting the top tricks available.

Suppose you are in 3NT, played by South (as in all bridge books), and you have this diamond suit:

♢ K 7 3

♢ A 10 9 6 2

You start with 'two top tricks in diamonds', the ♢A in your hand and the ♢K in dummy. No doubt you hope to score more diamond tricks eventually and this will form part of your 'plan'. For the moment, though, you have only two top tricks.

Let's say that this is your heart holding:

♡ Q J 3

♡ K 10 6

You have 'no top tricks in hearts' because the defenders hold the ace. Once you have knocked out the ♡A, you can establish two heart tricks. In your initial count of top tricks, though, you cannot count any from the heart suit.

Perhaps you also have this club suit:

♣ A Q

♣ K 4

Although you hold the ace, king and queen (three top cards) between the two hands, you have only two top club tricks. Once you have taken two club tricks, you will have no clubs left.

What do you make of this spade situation? How many top tricks do you have?

♠ A Q 8 3

♠ K 7 4

You would count this as three top tricks. You can score tricks with the ace, king and queen. If the defenders' spades break 3-3, you could actually score four spade tricks. At the start of the play, when you have little idea how the spades will break, you must count only three top tricks in spades.

You get the idea, then. You count the immediately available top tricks in each suit. The next stage is to add up those four numbers to get the total number of top tricks at the start. If you are in 3NT and you start with seven top tricks, you must look for a plan to create two more tricks. These will bring your total to nine. Of course, your plan must allow you to score these tricks before the defenders can take five tricks for themselves.

Let's look at a typical 3NT deal, counting the top tricks and making a plan for the extra tricks that you need:

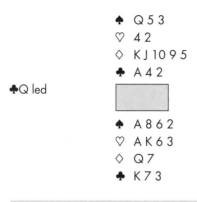

♣Q led

♠ Q 5 3
♡ 4 2
◇ K J 10 9 5
♣ A 4 2

♠ A 8 6 2
♡ A K 6 3
◇ Q 7
♣ K 7 3

West	North	East	South
			1NT
pass	3NT	all pass	

You open 1NT, showing 15-17 points. With 10 points and a useful five-card diamond suit, North is happy to raise to 3NT. There is no point bidding diamonds on the North hand because a nine-trick game (3NT) is usually much easier to make than an eleven-trick game (5◇). How will you play 3NT when West leads the ♣Q?

You will not fall off your chair when we tell you that your first task is to make a plan. In notrump, you start by counting your top winners. You have one in spades (the ♠A), two in hearts (the ♡A and ♡K), none in diamonds and two in clubs (the ♣A and ♣K). This is the summary of your top tricks:

Top Tricks: ♠ 1   ♡ 2   ◇ 0   ♣ 2   Total: 5

You have five top tricks and will need four more to make 3NT. What is your plan for creating these four extra tricks?

By establishing the diamond suit, you can easily set up four more tricks. To do this you will start by playing the ◇Q (a high card from the short side). The defenders will not help you by winning with the ◇A on the first round. If they win the second or third round, you will need an entry to dummy to reach the established diamonds. The ♣A will be needed as an entry, so you must win the first trick with the ♣K. How does the play go?

You win the first trick with the ♣K and play the ◇Q, which is allowed to win. When you play the ◇7 to dummy's ◇9, East wins with the ◇A. You will win East's return, cross to the ♣A and score a total of four diamond tricks for your contract.

> **PLAN: I will win with the ♣K and lead the ◇Q. I will play diamonds until they take the ◇A. I will win the return, cross to the ♣A and score four diamond tricks, bringing my total to nine.**

Bridge would be a dull old game if all 3NT contracts were as easy as that! In the next couple of chapters we will see how you can make many different 3NT contracts, with the aid of a few useful tips.

POINTS TO REMEMBER

- The first step in planning a notrump contract is to count your top tricks.

- An ace is always a top trick. When you hold the ace and king of a suit, the king will also be a top trick.

- Add up the top tricks in each suit to determine your 'Total Top Tricks'.

- If the total number of top tricks is fewer than the number you need for your chosen contract, you must make a plan to create one or more extra tricks.

- Your plan must allow you to score the extra tricks that you need before the defenders can beat the contract by scoring too many tricks their way.

7

HOLDING UP A STOPPER

In this chapter you can test yourself on several notrump contracts where you can succeed by holding up a stopper (a high card) in the suit that has been led. What does 'hold up' mean? It means that you refuse to play a high card, even though you could win the trick with it. In other words, you save your high card to win a subsequent trick.

Suppose West leads the ♠6 against 3NT and the suit lies like this:

♠ 10 5

♠ K J 9 6 4   ♠ Q 7 2

♠ A 8 3

West leads the ♠6 (it is normal to lead fourth-best unless you have a sequence of honors, such as KQJ, KQ10 or KJ10). East plays the ♠Q. If you win the first round with the ♠A, East will be able to return a spade if he wins a trick some time later, in a different suit. West will then score four tricks in spades, beating the contract. The same will happen if you win with the ♠A on the second round. East will still have a spade left and you will again lose four spade tricks

You will often have more chance of making 3NT if you allow the defenders to win the first two spade tricks. After you have won the third round with the ♠A, this will be the spade position:

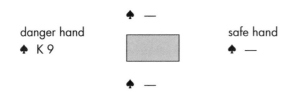

♠ —

danger hand   safe hand
♠ K 9   ♠ —

♠ —

East has no spades left! If he wins a trick in some other suit, he will not be able to return a spade. You may then be able to score nine or more tricks and make 3NT. For this reason East is known as the 'safe hand' or 'safe defender' here. If he gets the lead, he cannot damage you. West is the 'danger hand' or 'dangerous defender'. If he wins the lead he can cash two spade tricks.

That is the basic theory behind the 'hold-up play'. You refuse to play your ace until one defender has no more cards left in the suit. A good general rule is that you should hold up your ace for the first two rounds.

Let's put that spade suit into the context of a full deal. You are sitting South and hoping to make 3NT on this layout of the cards:

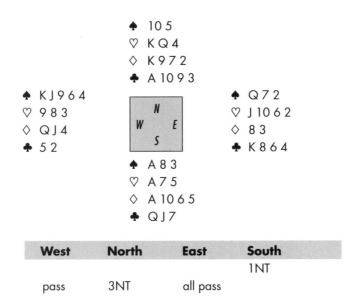

West	North	East	South
			1NT
pass	3NT	all pass	

West leads the ♠6, East playing the ♠Q. How will you play 3NT?

You have one top trick in spades (the ♠A) and three in hearts (the ♡AKQ). There are two further top tricks in diamonds (the ◇A and ◇K) and just one (the ♣A) in clubs. You start with this position:

Top Tricks: ♠ 1   ♡ 3   ◇ 2   ♣ 1   Total: 7

You have seven top tricks, so you will need two more to give you enough for 3NT. How will you play the contract?

Suppose you win the first trick with the ♠A and then lead the ♣Q for a finesse, hoping that West holds the ♣K. West and the dummy will play low and East will win with the ♣K. Curtains! East still has a spade to return. West scores four spade tricks and you are one down.

Instead, you should allow East's ♠Q to win the first trick, following with the ♠3. When he returns the ♠7, you play the ♠8 from your hand. West wins and plays a third round of spades, which you win with the ♠A. As before, you lead the ♣Q, playing low from the dummy. East wins but... what a difference! East has no spade to return. Whichever suit he plays next, you will win the trick and make nine tricks for the contract.

> **PLAN: I will hold up the ♠A for two rounds, winning the third round of spades. I will then lead the ♣Q and play a low card from dummy. If the club finesse loses to East's ♣K, he will probably have no spades left. I can win his return and score nine tricks.**

(Note that if East did have another spade left, the suit would break 4-4 and would not pose a problem. You would lose just three spades and one club.)

PROBLEM 41

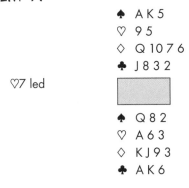

♥7 led

♠ A K 5
♥ 9 5
◇ Q 10 7 6
♣ J 8 3 2

♠ Q 8 2
♥ A 6 3
◇ K J 9 3
♣ A K 6

West	North	East	South
			1NT
pass	3NT	all pass	

Your 1NT opening bid shows 15-17 points and North has enough to raise to 3NT. How will you play the contract when West leads the ♥7?

Whether or not some strict-looking bridge teacher is standing behind you, watching your efforts, you should start by making a plan. You have these top tricks:

Top Tricks: ♠ 3   ♥ 1   ◇ 0   ♣ 2   Total: 6

You will need an extra three tricks to bring the total to nine. These can easily be established from the diamond suit, by knocking out the defenders ◇A. You must do your best to stop the defenders from scoring five tricks before you make nine. How will you play the contract?

SOLUTION 41

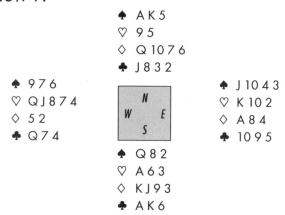

♠ A K 5
♡ 9 5
◇ Q 10 7 6
♣ J 8 3 2

♠ 9 7 6
♡ Q J 8 7 4
◇ 5 2
♣ Q 7 4

♠ J 10 4 3
♡ K 10 2
◇ A 8 4
♣ 10 9 5

♠ Q 8 2
♡ A 6 3
◇ K J 9 3
♣ A K 6

West leads the ♡7 against 3NT. Before playing a card from dummy, you must make a plan. In a notrump contract, the first step is to count your top tricks in each suit. Here you have been granted this situation:

Top Tricks: ♠ 3 ♡ 1 ◇ 0 ♣ 2 Total: 6

You can set up three extra tricks in diamonds by knocking out the defenders' ◇A. What will happen if you win the first round of hearts with the ♡A and play a diamond? It's not a difficult question to answer! East will win and return the ♡10. West will gleefully score four heart tricks and you will be one down.

It is normally right to hold up an ace for two rounds and that is exactly what you should do here. At Trick 1 East plays the ♡K and you must allow this card to win, following with the ♡3. When East returns the ♡10, you play the ♡6 from your hand. You are following the general guideline that you should hold up an ace for two rounds.

The defenders play a third round of hearts and you win with the ace. When you play the diamond suit, East will take his ◇A at some stage. He will then have no heart to play (unless hearts break 4-4 and pose you no problem). Suppose he switches to the ♣10. You will win with the ♣A and score nine tricks.

Are you wondering what would have happened if West held the ◇A alongside a five-card heart suit? You would have gone down, yes, but in that case there was no way to make the contract. By holding up the ♡A twice, you gave yourself the chance of making 3NT when East held the ◇A.

> **PLAN: I will hold up the ♡A until the third round, allowing the defenders to win the first two heart tricks. I will then play diamonds, hoping that it is East (the safe hand) who holds the ◇A.**

PROBLEM 42

♠ Q 8 4
♡ A 8 2
◊ J 10 4
♣ A Q 10 4

♡5 led

♠ A K J 7
♡ 10 6
◊ A Q 9 5
♣ J 9 5

West	North	East	South
			1NT
pass	3NT	all pass	

West leads the ♡5 against 3NT. Partner will not be expecting you to go down, with his 13 points opposite your 15-17 point 1NT opening. How will you plan the contract?

You start with these top tricks:

Top Tricks: ♠ 4   ♡ 1   ◊ 1   ♣ 1   **Total: 7**

You have seven top tricks and will therefore need two more to bring you to the finishing line. What is the safest way to set up these tricks? You need to choose a plan that will not run the risk of the defenders scoring five tricks before you can make the contract.

The diamond and club suits offer you the chance to create more tricks. Which of these suits will you tackle first? How will you play the contract?

POINT TO REMEMBER

When you are deciding whether or not to hold up an ace, it makes no difference whether the ace is in your hand or in the dummy.

SOLUTION 42

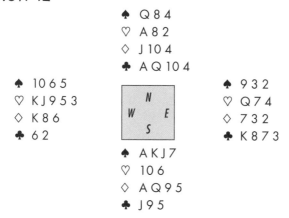

```
              ♠ Q 8 4
              ♡ A 8 2
              ◇ J 10 4
              ♣ A Q 10 4
♠ 10 6 5                        ♠ 9 3 2
♡ K J 9 5 3      N              ♡ Q 7 4
◇ K 8 6      W       E          ◇ 7 3 2
♣ 6 2            S              ♣ K 8 7 3
              ♠ A K J 7
              ♡ 10 6
              ◇ A Q 9 5
              ♣ J 9 5
```

West leads the ♡5 against 3NT. This is your tally of top tricks:

Top Tricks: ♠ 4 ♡ 1 ◇ 1 ♣ 1 Total: 7

Suppose you take a finesse at some stage in one of the minor suits. Even if the finesse loses to the king, you will establish two extra tricks in the suit — enough to bring your total to nine. All you have to worry about is the risk that the defenders will score five tricks if your chosen finesse (in diamonds or clubs) fails. How can you prevent this from happening?

You will not be surprised to hear that the first step is a hold-up play. As usual, you should hold up the ♡A until the third round. When you play the ♡2 from dummy, East wins with the ♡Q and returns the ♡7. West plays the ♡J and you duck once more in the dummy. You then win the third round with the ♡A. What next?

Suppose you decide to take the diamond finesse, leading the ◇J and playing low from the South hand. Disaster! The finesse will lose and West will cash two further winners in hearts to put you one down. You finessed into the danger hand, into the hand of the defender who had hearts to cash.

Instead you should lead a low spade to your ♠A. You then lead the ♣J, playing the ♣4 from dummy. This finesse also loses but it is into the safe hand. East has no heart to play and nine tricks are yours. (Because you are going to finesse in clubs, note that you should discard a diamond from your hand on the ♡A.)

> **PLAN: I will hold up the ♡A until the third round, play a small spade to the ♠A and finesse clubs into the safe (East) hand.**

POINT TO REMEMBER

After a hold-up play, one defender is 'dangerous' (he has winners to play), the other is 'safe' (he has no cards left in the suit that was led). You should prefer to finesse into the safe hand.

PROBLEM 43

```
              ♠  10 3
              ♡  7 6 2
              ◇  A Q J 10 4
              ♣  K 7 4
♠6 led
              ┌──────────┐
              │          │
              └──────────┘
              ♠  K 9 4
              ♡  A K 8
              ◇  8 7 2
              ♣  A J 5 2
```

West	North	East	South
			1NT
pass	3NT	all pass	

West leads the ♠6 against 3NT and East wins with the ♠A. What is your plan for the contract when East returns the ♠8?

How many top tricks do you have? You can count one in spades after East has taken his ace. You also have two in hearts, one in diamonds and two more in clubs. This is the position:

Top Tricks: ♠ 1 ♡ 2 ◇ 1 ♣ 2 Total: 6

You need to find three extra tricks from somewhere. You have a chance of extra tricks in both diamonds and clubs. How will you play the contract?

POINT TO REMEMBER

The dangerous case in most 3NT contracts is when the opening leader holds five cards in the suit led and his partner holds two or three cards. By holding up your stopper, you can remove the cards in the hand of one of the defenders. He is then known as the safe hand. It will be safe for you to lose a trick to that defender.

SOLUTION 43

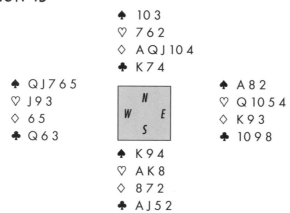

```
              ♠ 10 3
              ♡ 7 6 2
              ◇ A Q J 10 4
              ♣ K 7 4
♠ Q J 7 6 5                      ♠ A 8 2
♡ J 9 3          N              ♡ Q 10 5 4
◇ 6 5         W     E           ◇ K 9 3
♣ Q 6 3          S              ♣ 10 9 8
              ♠ K 9 4
              ♡ A K 8
              ◇ 8 7 2
              ♣ A J 5 2
```

West leads the ♠6 against 3NT, East winning with the ♠A and returning the ♠8. You can see these top tricks:

Top Tricks: ♠ 1   ♡ 2   ◇ 1   ♣ 2   Total: 6

You have a good chance of creating extra tricks from the diamond suit. If West holds the ◇K, you can finesse successfully against it. Even if the diamond finesse loses, you will still score four diamond tricks. What you cannot afford is to take a losing diamond finesse when East still has a spade to return. How can you avoid this unwelcome possibility?

You must hold up your ♣K until the third round. When East returns the ♠8, you play the ♠9. West wins with the ♠J and continues the spade suit. You win with the ♠K and lead the ◇2 to dummy's ◇Q. If East wins with the ◇K, he will have no spade left to play. You will win whatever he returns and score your nine tricks. The contract is yours.

If the ◇Q wins the first round of diamonds, either because West holds the ◇K or East chooses not to win with the ◇K, you return to your hand with the ♡K and lead a diamond to the ◇J. Even in the case where West holds four diamonds including the king, you can take three diamond finesses and make an overtrick.

> **PLAN: I will hold up the ♠K until the third round. I will finesse the ◇Q (and then the ◇J if the ◇Q wins), scoring three or four extra diamond tricks.**

POINT TO REMEMBER

When you have a combination such as AQJ104, you can often take several finesses in the suit. That is the meaning of the term 'repeat finesse'.

PROBLEM 44

♠ K 8 4
♡ Q 4
◇ A K Q 10 6
♣ 10 3 2

♡6 led

```
          ┌─────────┐
          │         │
          └─────────┘
```

♠ A J 5
♡ A 8 3
◇ J 9 8 3
♣ J 5 4

West	North	East	South
	1◇	pass	2NT
pass	3NT	all pass	

West leads the ♡6 against 3NT. You try your luck with dummy's ♡Q but East covers with the ♡K. What is your plan for making the game?

You start with these top tricks:

Top Tricks: ♠ 2   ♡ 1   ◇ 5   ♣ 0   Total: 8

You need only one more trick to make the contract. What plan will you make?

POINT TO REMEMBER

The main purpose of a hold-up play is to make one of the defenders 'safe', by removing his cards in the suit that was led. There is no purpose in a hold-up play unless you may possibly benefit from it. For example, you may be able to set up extra tricks by letting the safe hand win the lead.

SOLUTION 44

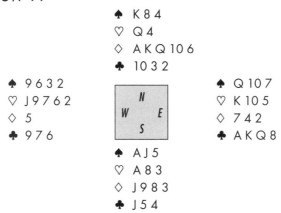

```
              ♠ K 8 4
              ♡ Q 4
              ◇ A K Q 10 6
              ♣ 10 3 2
♠ 9 6 3 2                         ♠ Q 10 7
♡ J 9 7 6 2        N             ♡ K 10 5
◇ 5            W       E         ◇ 7 4 2
♣ 9 7 6            S             ♣ A K Q 8
              ♠ A J 5
              ♡ A 8 3
              ◇ J 9 8 3
              ♣ J 5 4
```

West leads the ♡6 against 3NT. You try dummy's ♡Q but East covers with the ♡K. How will you play the contract? You have these top tricks at the start:

Top Tricks: ♠ 2   ♡ 1   ◇ 5   ♣ 0   Total: 8

Suppose you look only at the heart suit, not bothering to make a plan for the contract as a whole. 'That's lucky. I've just been reading a book that explained about holding up aces. Apparently, you need to hold up the ace for two rounds.' You play low from hand at Trick 1, but East gives you a nasty surprise by playing the ♣A, ♣K and ♣Q. He then puts the ♣8 on the table and you are one down!

Of course, you would not play the contract this way. You would start by making a plan. You have eight top tricks and the only chance of a ninth trick is to finesse the ♠J, hoping that East holds the ♠Q. This gives you a 50% chance of success.

Should you hold up the ♡A? There are two good reasons why you should not do this. The first is that you have no club stopper and there would be a risk of East switching to clubs. The second reason is that there is no point in holding up the ♡A anyway! Suppose the defenders continued to play hearts, not realizing that they could take four club tricks. How would that help you? You would still need the 50% finesse of the ♠J to give you a ninth trick.

You should win the first heart and play five rounds of diamonds, discarding a club from your hand. You then go for your 50% chance, leading the ♣4 to your ♠J.

> **PLAN: I will win with the ♡A, play the diamonds and finesse the ♠J. When East holds the ♠Q, I will make the game.**

POINT TO REMEMBER

Do not hold up an ace when the defenders may be able to score too many tricks by switching to a different suit. Nor should you hold up an ace when there is no purpose in doing so.

PROBLEM 45

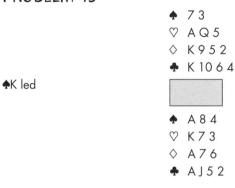

♠ 7 3
♡ A Q 5
◇ K 9 5 2
♣ K 10 6 4

♠K led

♠ A 8 4
♡ K 7 3
◇ A 7 6
♣ A J 5 2

West	North	East	South
			1NT
pass	3NT	all pass	

West leads the ♠K against your contract of 3NT. How will you plan the play? You start with these top tricks:

Top Tricks: ♠ 1   ♡ 3   ◇ 2   ♣ 2   Total: 8

You have eight top tricks and will need one more to make your game. How will you play the hand to give yourself the best chance of making nine tricks before the defenders can score the five tricks that they need?

POINT TO REMEMBER

The intention behind a hold-up play is to remove all the cards in that suit from one of the defenders. He then becomes the 'safe hand' or 'safe defender'. You will not mind if he wins a trick while you are setting up the extra tricks that you need.

SOLUTION 45

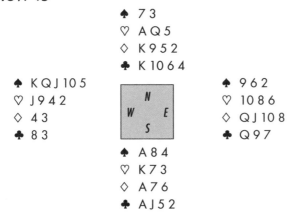

```
                ♠ 7 3
                ♡ A Q 5
                ◇ K 9 5 2
                ♣ K 10 6 4
  ♠ K Q J 10 5           ♠ 9 6 2
  ♡ J 9 4 2      N        ♡ 10 8 6
  ◇ 4 3      W       E    ◇ Q J 10 8
  ♣ 8 3          S        ♣ Q 9 7
                ♠ A 8 4
                ♡ K 7 3
                ◇ A 7 6
                ♣ A J 5 2
```

West leads the ♠K against your 3NT contract. You start to make a plan for the contract, finding that you have these top tricks:

Top Tricks: ♠ 1   ♡ 3   ◇ 2   ♣ 2   Total: 8

You need only one extra trick and that can be found in the club suit. You have a 'two-way finesse' there. What does that mean? It means that you can choose to finesse against either defender for the missing ♣Q. If you think that West holds the ♣Q, you will play the ♣A and then lead the ♣2 to dummy's ♣10. If instead you think East has the ♣Q, you can play the ♣K and then lead the ♣4 to your ♣J.

Which way do you think you should finesse in clubs on this particular hand? Remember to think about the whole deal, not just the club suit in isolation.

The point is that you can afford to lose the club finesse, provided the defenders cannot then take enough tricks to beat the contract. If a club finesse fails, the remaining cards in the suit will give you the extra trick that you need. The correct play is to hold up the ♠A until the third round, to exhaust East's spades when West has five spades to East's three. You then play the ♣A and lead the ♣2 to the ♣10. You don't care whether the finesse wins or not! When the cards lie as above, the finesse will lose but East will have no spade to return. Nine tricks are yours.

If instead you unwisely played the ♣K and then finessed the ♣J, you would go down when West held the ♣Q and could cash two more spade tricks.

PLAN: I will hold up the ♠A until the third round and then finesse clubs into the safe (East) hand.

POINT TO REMEMBER

Quite often you cannot tell the best play in a suit just by looking at that suit alone. You must consider the whole deal and whether one particular defender is dangerous and cannot be allowed to win a trick.

PROBLEM 46

♠ K 10 7
♡ 5 3 2
♢ Q J 10 9 5
♣ A 8

♡Q led

♠ A 9 4
♡ A K 7
♢ 7 6 2
♣ K J 6 2

West	North	East	South
			1NT
pass	3NT	all pass	

How do you play this contract when West leads the ♡Q?

For the first time in this chapter, you have two stoppers in the suit that has been led. When you come to make a detailed plan, you may have to consider whether it is worth holding up on the first round of hearts, even though you have two stoppers.

Let's see how many top tricks we have at the start:

Top Tricks: ♠ 2   ♡ 2   ♢ 0   ♣ 2   Total: 6

Three ace-king combinations give you six top tricks. The three extra tricks that you need to increase this total to nine can be obtained by establishing the diamond suit. Since you have two diamond stoppers to knock out, the defenders will win the lead twice in the suit. Will that give them a chance to score three heart tricks (along with the two top diamonds) to beat the contract? That depends on how you intend to play!

What is your plan?

SOLUTION 46

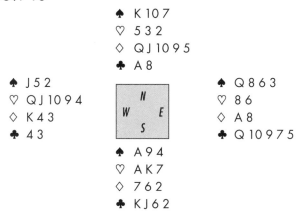

```
              ♠ K 10 7
              ♡ 5 3 2
              ◇ Q J 10 9 5
              ♣ A 8
♠ J 5 2                          ♠ Q 8 6 3
♡ Q J 10 9 4      N             ♡ 8 6
◇ K 4 3        W     E          ◇ A 8
♣ 4 3             S             ♣ Q 10 9 7 5
              ♠ A 9 4
              ♡ A K 7
              ◇ 7 6 2
              ♣ K J 6 2
```

West leads the ♡Q against 3NT and this is your top trick position:

Top Tricks: ♠ 2   ♡ 2   ◇ 0   ♣ 2   Total: 6

Three extra tricks from the diamond suit will bring your total to nine, but you must try to ensure that the defenders cannot score three hearts and two diamonds first.

Let's see what will happen if you win the first trick with one of your heart honors. When you then play a diamond, East will win with the ◇A and lead another heart. It will not do you any good to start thinking of a hold-up in hearts at this stage. Even if you delay winning your other heart honor until the third round, you will still go down. When West wins with the ◇K, he will cash his remaining hearts.

To make the contract you must allow West's ♡Q to win the first trick — holding up even though you have two stoppers in the suit. You win the second round of hearts and play a diamond to the queen. What a difference! When East wins with the ◇A he has no hearts left. You will win his return in a different suit and continue to play diamonds, knocking out West's ◇K. When you regain the lead, you will score three diamond tricks in addition to the top tricks that you were dealt. The contract will be yours.

> **PLAN: I will duck the first trick, allowing West's ♡Q to win. When I win the next heart, East will have no hearts left (in the dangerous case where hearts are 5-2). I can then set up the diamonds safely unless West holds both the ◇A and ◇K.**

POINT TO REMEMBER

When you have two stoppers to knock out (the ◇A and ◇K on this deal), it can be right to hold up even with two stoppers in the suit led. The aim, as always, is to remove one defender's cards in that suit.

PROBLEM 47

♠ 8 7
♡ 10 6 5
◇ K Q 9 8 4
♣ K J 2

♠2 led

♠ A 10 4
♡ A 7 2
◇ J 10 7 5
♣ A Q 6

West	North	East	South
			1NT
pass	3NT	all pass	

West, who is playing fourth-best leads, chooses the ♠2 as his opening lead. How will you play 3NT?

You start the campaign with these top tricks:

Top Tricks: ♠ **1** ♡ **1** ◇ **0** ♣ **3** **Total: 5**

Only five top tricks, it's true, but there is an easy source of four extra tricks in diamonds. All you need to consider is how to prevent the opponents from scoring five tricks before you can score your nine. What will your plan be to do this? The first question to ask is: 'Should I hold up the ♠A?'

POINT TO REMEMBER

Choosing the correct line of play in a 3NT contract may depend on reading how many cards the opening leader has in the suit he has led. If he holds five cards, and you have only one stopper, then his suit may pose a serious threat. Unless a switch to another suit would be threatening, you should usually hold up your stopper in the suit led.

SOLUTION 47

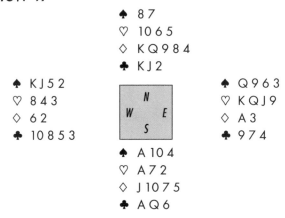

```
              ♠ 8 7
              ♡ 10 6 5
              ◇ K Q 9 8 4
              ♣ K J 2
♠ K J 5 2                        ♠ Q 9 6 3
♡ 8 4 3          N              ♡ K Q J 9
◇ 6 2         W     E           ◇ A 3
♣ 10 8 5 3        S             ♣ 9 7 4
              ♠ A 10 4
              ♡ A 7 2
              ◇ J 10 7 5
              ♣ A Q 6
```

West leads the ♠2 against 3NT and you have these top tricks:

Top Tricks: ♠ 1   ♡ 1   ◇ 0   ♣ 3   Total: 5

Four tricks in diamonds will bring your total to the nine that you need. Make your own decision now, whether you should hold up the ♠A. When you have done that, we will see how the original declarer went down in the contract.

The original declarer did not make a proper plan and decided that he would hold up the ♠A. When the ♠Q was allowed to win, East was quick to switch to the ♡K. The contract could not then be made, whatever declarer did. When diamonds were eventually played, East won with the ◇A and scored three heart tricks. One spade, three hearts and one diamond put the contract one down.

'If you win the first trick with the ♠A, you make it,' North observed. When you set up the diamond suit, they can take only three spade tricks and a diamond.'

Are you wondering how declarer could tell that spades were breaking 4-4? It is because West led the ♠2. If this was his fourth-best card in the suit, it was impossible for him to hold a fifth-best card! If West held a five-card suit, such as ♠KJ652, he would lead the fourth-best ♠5 and would still have the ♠2 in his hand. When he leads the ♠2, you can place him with four spades.

When spades break 4-4, they pose no threat; nothing can be gained by holding up the ♠A. You should win immediately and knock out the ◇A.

> **PLAN: I will win the spade lead immediately and establish the diamonds. West's ♠2 lead makes it very likely that spades are 4-4. In that case I will lose just three spades and a diamond.**

POINT TO REMEMBER

After West leads, if you can see all the lower spot cards in your own hand or dummy, you can assume that West has led from a four-card suit.

PROBLEM 48

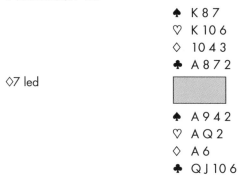

♠ K 8 7
♡ K 10 6
◇ 10 4 3
♣ A 8 7 2

◇7 led

♠ A 9 4 2
♡ A Q 2
◇ A 6
♣ Q J 10 6

West	North	East	South
			1NT
pass	3NT	all pass	

West leads the ◇7 against 3NT. How will you play the contract?

Before playing to the first trick, you pause to count your top tricks. You have two in spades and three in hearts. In diamonds and clubs you can count just one top winner for the ace of the suit. This is the situation:

Top Tricks: ♠ 2   ♡ 3   ◇ 1   ♣ 1   Total: 7

The two extra tricks that you need will surely have to come from the club suit. How will you play the hand? Is there anything you can do to reduce the risk that the opponents will score enough tricks to beat the contract before you can make the game?

SOLUTION 48

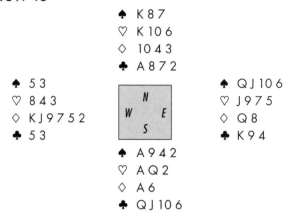

```
              ♠ K 8 7
              ♡ K 10 6
              ◇ 10 4 3
              ♣ A 8 7 2
  ♠ 5 3                        ♠ Q J 10 6
  ♡ 8 4 3          N           ♡ J 9 7 5
  ◇ K J 9 7 5 2  W   E         ◇ Q 8
  ♣ 5 3            S           ♣ K 9 4
              ♠ A 9 4 2
              ♡ A Q 2
              ◇ A 6
              ♣ Q J 10 6
```

West leads the ◇7 against 3NT this is the top trick position:

Top Tricks: ♠ 2   ♡ 3   ◇ 1   ♣ 1   Total: 7

You need another two tricks from somewhere. A club finesse will yield two extra tricks, even if the finesse fails. The risk is that the finesse will fail and East will return a diamond, allowing West to score enough diamond tricks to beat you. You would like to hold up the ◇A for two rounds, which would remove East's diamonds in the dangerous case when diamonds break 5-3. You cannot hold up for two rounds when you hold only ◇A6. What else can you try?

You can hold up your ace for one round! You will still go down when the club finesse loses and diamonds break 5-3, it's true, but in that case there was no way to make 3NT. By holding up the ◇A for one round, you will at least make the contract when diamonds happen to break 6-2. How does the play go?

When West leads the ◇7, East plays the ◇Q and you allow this card to win. East returns the ◇8 and you win with the ◇A. You lead the ♣Q, playing low from dummy, and (oh dear) East wins with the ♣K. You brace yourself for another diamond but East switches to the ♠Q. Excellent! East had no diamond to return after your hold-up of the ◇A. You now score nine tricks, making the contract.

> **PLAN: I will hold up the ◇A on the first round and win the second round of diamonds. I will then finesse in clubs, leading the ♣Q and playing low in dummy. When diamonds are 6-2, or the club finesse wins, I will make the contract.**

POINT TO REMEMBER

When you hold a doubleton ace in the suit led against 3NT, it can still be worthwhile to hold up the ace for one round. This will exhaust your right-hand opponent's cards in the suit when he began with a doubleton.

PROBLEM 49

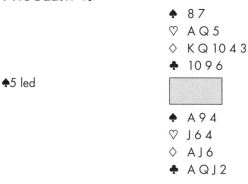

♠5 led

```
        ♠ 8 7
        ♡ A Q 5
        ◊ K Q 10 4 3
        ♣ 10 9 6

        ♠ A 9 4
        ♡ J 6 4
        ◊ A J 6
        ♣ A Q J 2
```

West	North	East	South
			1NT
pass	3NT	all pass	

West leads the ♠5 against 3NT, East playing the ♠Q. How will you play the contract?

When you count your top tricks, you find this is the position:

Top Tricks: ♠ 1   ♡ 1   ◊ 5   ♣ 1   Total: 8

It could be worse. You have eight top tricks and therefore need only one more to make the game. When you come to planning your play of the hand, you must look for the safest way to create the one extra trick that you need. Which suit offers you a safe route to '3NT bid and made'? Which suit risks going down?

SOLUTION 49

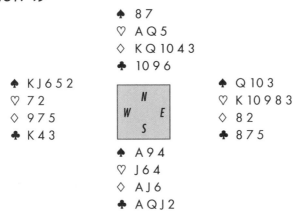

```
              ♠ 8 7
              ♡ A Q 5
              ◇ K Q 10 4 3
              ♣ 10 9 6
  ♠ K J 6 5 2                ♠ Q 10 3
  ♡ 7 2            N         ♡ K 10 9 8 3
  ◇ 9 7 5      W     E       ◇ 8 2
  ♣ K 4 3          S         ♣ 8 7 5
              ♠ A 9 4
              ♡ J 6 4
              ◇ A J 6
              ♣ A Q J 2
```

West leads the ♠5 against your 3NT, East playing the ♠Q. What is your plan? You start with eight top tricks at your disposal:

Top Tricks: ♠ 1   ♡ 1   ◇ 5   ♣ 1   Total: 8

There are two suits that offer you a chance to create extra tricks. You can finesse against the king in the club suit. If East holds the ♣K, you will score three extra club tricks. If West holds the ♣K, you will lose a trick to the ♣K, but you would still set up two extra tricks in the suit.

Another option is to finesse the ♡Q. If this finesse is successful you will make the extra trick that you need. If the heart finesse loses, you will still score an extra trick (with the ♡J). The question is this: should you finesse in clubs or in hearts?

You start by holding up the ♠A until the third round. In the dangerous case where spades started 5-3, East now has no spades left. He is the safe hand.

If you take a club finesse now, it will be into the danger hand (West). If it loses, you will go down! West will win and score two more spade tricks.

If instead you take a heart finesse, it will be into the safe hand (East). Even if it loses, you will still make the contract!

The club finesse gives you a 50% chance of making the contract — you will need the finesse to win. The heart finesse gives you a 100% chance of making the contract — you will make it whether the finesse wins or not. What more could you want?

> **PLAN: I will hold up the ♠A for two rounds and then lead a low heart to dummy's ♡Q, finessing into the safe (East) hand.**

POINT TO REMEMBER

When you have possible finesses in two different suits, take the finesse that will be into the safe hand.

PROBLEM 50 (a little more difficult)

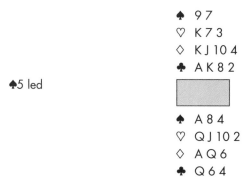

♠ 9 7
♡ K 7 3
♢ K J 10 4
♣ A K 8 2

♠5 led

♠ A 8 4
♡ Q J 10 2
♢ A Q 6
♣ Q 6 4

West	North	East	South
			1NT
pass	3NT	all pass	

How will you play 3NT when West leads the ♠5, East playing the ♠Q? Your partner will be surprised if you go down, with 14 points in the dummy facing your 15-17 point 1NT. How many top tricks do you have?

For the second problem in a row, you have eight top tricks:

Top Tricks: ♠ 1   ♡ 0   ♢ 4   ♣ 3   Total: 8

How many spades is West likely to have? The ♠5 is his fourth-best spade and the defenders also hold the ♠3 and the ♠2. It is likely that West will hold at least one of these cards. Most of the time he will hold five spades and East will hold three. What plan will you make?

The heart suit offers you the chance to set up three extra tricks. Are you planning to rely solely on that source?

SOLUTION 50

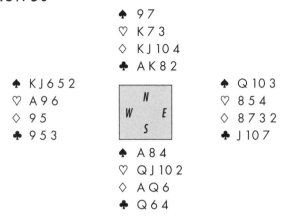

```
              ♠ 9 7
              ♡ K 7 3
              ◇ K J 10 4
              ♣ A K 8 2

♠ K J 6 5 2                    ♠ Q 10 3
♡ A 9 6          N            ♡ 8 5 4
◇ 9 5         W     E         ◇ 8 7 3 2
♣ 9 5 3          S            ♣ J 10 7

              ♠ A 8 4
              ♡ Q J 10 2
              ◇ A Q 6
              ♣ Q 6 4
```

West leads the ♠5 against 3NT, East playing the ♠Q. You have these top tricks:

Top Tricks: ♠ 1   ♡ 0   ◇ 4   ♣ 3   Total: 8

The heart suit will give you three extra tricks, once you have knocked out the defenders' ♡A. By holding up the ♠A for two rounds, you would make the contract if you subsequently played on hearts and it was East (the safe hand) who happened to hold the ♡A. Do you see another suit that offers a chance of an extra trick? You will score a fourth trick from the clubs if the suit breaks 3-3. The ♣AKQ will draw the defenders' cards and the ♣8 will then be good. How should the play go?

The first step is to hold up the ♠A for two rounds. East wins the first trick and returns the ♠10. This suggests that he started with three spades (or possibly only two) and is returning the higher of his remaining cards. You play the ♠8 from your hand, holding up the ♠A for the second time. When the defenders play a third round of spades, you throw the ♡3 from dummy and win with the ♠A. What now?

Before playing a heart, hoping that East (the safe hand) will win the trick, you should test the clubs. You play the ♣Q and ♣A, everyone following. You continue with the ♣K and both defenders follow! Yes, the suit breaks 3-3 and the ♣8 is your ninth trick. You score one spade, four clubs and four diamonds, making 3NT.

If you had played a heart, instead of testing the clubs first, you would have gone down. West would have won with the ♡A and taken two more spade tricks.

> **PLAN: I will hold up the ♠A until the third round. I will then test the clubs. If they break 3-3, I am home. Otherwise, I will play a heart, hoping that East (the safe hand) holds the ♡A.**

POINT TO REMEMBER

You can often combine two chances of making a contract. Here you get home on a 3-3 club break or if the safe hand holds the ♡A.

ESTABLISHING SUITS IN NOTRUMP

In Chapter 5 we looked at how you can establish a suit when you are playing in a trump contract. With ◊AK865 in dummy opposite ◊72, for example, you could play the ◊A and ◊K and then ruff a diamond in your hand. If the suit broke 3-3, dummy's remaining cards would be established. If instead the diamonds broke 4-2, you would need one more ruff to establish dummy's last card in the suit.

The situation is a bit different at notrump. Since you cannot take any ruffs, you will often have to give up one or more tricks to the defenders, eventually establishing the remainder of the suit.

Let's say you are playing in 3NT with the diamond suit mentioned above:

◇ A K 8 6 5

◇ J 9 4   ◇ Q 10 3

◇ 7 2

Suppose you played the ◇A and ◇K, continuing with the ◇5 from dummy and giving away that trick. When the suit broke 3-3, the ◇8 and ◇6 would both be good. However, you would need an entry in some other suit to reach the two established cards. If there was no such entry, you would be sunk.

There is a better way of playing a suit like this. You are intending to duck a round of diamonds anyway — in other words, to play a low diamond from both hands, allowing the defenders to win the trick. In that case you might as well duck the first round of diamonds. You lead the ◇7, West following with the ◇4, and play the ◇5 from dummy. East wins with the ◇10 and these cards now remain in the diamond suit:

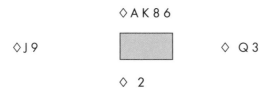

◇ A K 8 6

◇ J 9   ◇ Q 3

◇ 2

You see how well that works? You can now cross to the ◇A and play the ◇K. When the suit breaks 3-3, as before, you are now in the right hand to score tricks with the ◇8 and ◇6. You will not need an entry to dummy in some different suit.

POINT TO REMEMBER

> When dummy has a suit such as AKxxx or AKxxxx opposite two low cards in your hand, it can be a good idea to duck the first round. You can then cross to dummy on the second round.

Another way that you can establish a suit in a notrump contract is by taking finesses in the suit. Look at this complete deal:

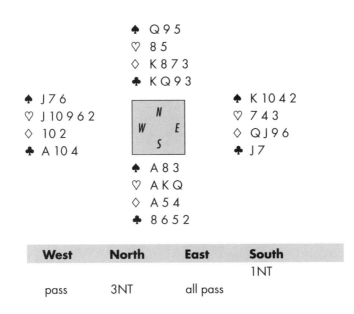

	♠ Q 9 5	
	♡ 8 5	
	◇ K 8 7 3	
	♣ K Q 9 3	

♠ J 7 6		♠ K 10 4 2
♡ J 10 9 6 2		♡ 7 4 3
◇ 10 2		◇ Q J 9 6
♣ A 10 4		♣ J 7

	♠ A 8 3	
	♡ A K Q	
	◇ A 5 4	
	♣ 8 6 5 2	

West	North	East	South
			1NT
pass	3NT	all pass	

West leads the ♡J against 3NT and you see you have one top trick in spades, three in hearts and two in diamonds. You start with this position:

Top Tricks: ♠ 1   ♡ 3   ◇ 2   ♣ 0   Total: 6

You have six top tricks, so you will need three more to give you enough for 3NT. How will you play the contract?

You might make one extra trick in spades (by leading towards the ♠Q), or one extra trick in diamonds, by finding a 3-3 break and establishing the thirteenth card in the suit. Even if both those chances came off, you would still be looking for one more trick! Meanwhile, the club suit offers you the chance to score the three extra tricks you need. You will lead twice towards dummy's ♣KQ93, hoping that West holds the ♣A and that the suit breaks 3-2. How does the play go?

You win the first trick with the ♡Q and lead the ♣2, West playing the ♣4. When you play dummy's ♣Q, this wins the trick. You return to your hand with the ◇A and lead the ♣5 (again leading from the weaker side of the suit towards the stronger side). West follows with the ♣10 and you play the ♣K. It wins the trick and East follows with the ♣J. There is now only one club out. You lead a third round of clubs from dummy and West wins with the ♣A. Whatever he plays next, you will have nine tricks to take, including the three extra tricks that you managed to establish in clubs.

> **PLAN: I will win the heart lead and lead the ♣2 towards dummy's honors. If the ♣Q wins, I will return to the ◇A and lead the ♣5 towards dummy. When West holds the ♣A and clubs break 3-2, I will score the three extra tricks that I need.**

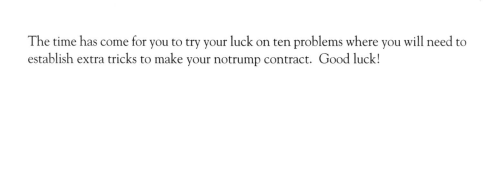

The time has come for you to try your luck on ten problems where you will need to establish extra tricks to make your notrump contract. Good luck!

PROBLEM 51

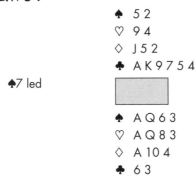

♠ 5 2
♡ 9 4
◇ J 5 2
♣ A K 9 7 5 4

♠7 led

♠ A Q 6 3
♡ A Q 8 3
◇ A 10 4
♣ 6 3

West	North	East	South
			1NT
pass	3NT	all pass	

North raises to 3NT, remembering the general guideline that it is easier to make nine tricks in notrump than eleven with clubs or diamonds as trumps. Some teachers say: 'Diamonds are for your fingers and clubs are for the golf course!' West leads the ♠7 against 3NT and East plays the ♠10. What is your plan for the contract?

You start by counting your top tricks: after the spade lead you can count two top tricks in spades. You have one in hearts and one in diamonds. In clubs, you have only two top tricks although you are doubtless hoping to make several more club tricks eventually.

You start with this position:

Top Tricks: ♣ 2   ♡ 1   ◇ 1   ♣ 2   **Total: 6**

You need three extra tricks from somewhere. Hearts and diamonds offer you limited prospects at best. You will surely need to establish the club suit.

POINT TO REMEMBER

> If the opening lead runs into your ace-queen combination, you are certain to score tricks with both the ace and the queen. You can therefore count two top tricks in the suit when you make your plan.

SOLUTION 51

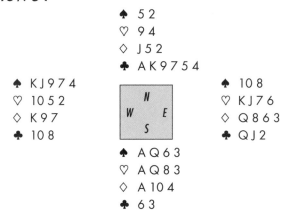

```
                ♠ 5 2
                ♡ 9 4
                ◇ J 5 2
                ♣ A K 9 7 5 4
 ♠ K J 9 7 4                      ♠ 10 8
 ♡ 10 5 2         N               ♡ K J 7 6
 ◇ K 9 7      W       E           ◇ Q 8 6 3
 ♣ 10 8           S               ♣ Q J 2
                ♠ A Q 6 3
                ♡ A Q 8 3
                ◇ A 10 4
                ♣ 6 3
```

West leads the ♠7 against 3NT and East plays the ♠10. West must have led away from the ♠K and this has given you two certain tricks in the spade suit. You are entitled to count these in your summary of the top tricks:

Top Tricks: ♠ 2   ♡ 1   ◇ 1   ♣ 2   Total: 6

You need three extra tricks from the club suit and this will be possible if the defenders' clubs break 3-2. You need to make sure that you can reach the established cards in clubs after you have set up the suit. What will you do at Trick 2 after winning East's ♠10 with the ♠Q?

Suppose you cross to the ♣K and play the ♣A, both defenders following suit. You can establish the suit by leading a third round of clubs, allowing the defenders to win the trick. How will you then get back to dummy?

The answer is that you will not be able to get back to dummy! You will score only two club tricks and go down in your contract. With a suit like this, you must duck the very first round of clubs. You lead the ♣3 and play the ♣4 (or some other low club) from dummy. East will win this trick but you are now going to make the contract. You will win whatever card East returns and lead the ♣6 to dummy's ♣K. Both defenders follow and there is only one club still out. Dummy's remaining ♣A975 will give you four more tricks, enough for the contract.

> **PLAN: I will win with the ♠Q and duck a round of clubs (in other words, play a low club from both hands). I will win the defenders' return and cross to the ♣K. If clubs break 3-2, I will make five club tricks, which are enough for game.**

POINT TO REMEMBER

When you want to set up a long suit in dummy and the dummy is short of entries, it is often a good move to duck the first round of the suit.

PROBLEM 52

♠ K 5 2
♡ 9 4
◇ A Q J 10 2
♣ 9 7 5

♡K led

♠ A 9 6 3
♡ A 8 5
◇ 7 4 3
♣ A K 6

West	North	East	South
			1NT
pass	3NT	all pass	

West leads the ♡K against 3NT. You can count these top tricks:

Top Tricks: ♠ 2   ♡ 1   ◇ 1   ♣ 2   Total: 6

You have six top tricks and hope to make several more from dummy's diamond suit. Even if East holds the ◇K, you will still make four diamond tricks (three extra tricks) and this will bring your total to nine. How can you reduce the risk of losing too many heart tricks if the diamond finesse fails?

POINT TO REMEMBER

When you are not sure whether a finesse in dummy's long suit will win or lose, look for a plan that may work whichever defender holds the missing high card.

SOLUTION 52

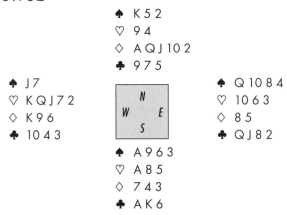

```
              ♠ K 5 2
              ♡ 9 4
              ◇ A Q J 10 2
              ♣ 9 7 5
♠ J 7                          ♠ Q 10 8 4
♡ K Q J 7 2        N           ♡ 10 6 3
◇ K 9 6        W       E       ◇ 8 5
♣ 10 4 3           S           ♣ Q J 8 2
              ♠ A 9 6 3
              ♡ A 8 5
              ◇ 7 4 3
              ♣ A K 6
```

West leads the ♡K against 3NT and you start with these top tricks:

Top Tricks: ♠ 2   ♡ 1   ◇ 1   ♣ 2   Total: 6

You need three more tricks and these will come from the diamond suit, even if East holds the ◇K and you are destined to lose a diamond trick. What you cannot afford is for East to win with the ◇K and for the defenders to then cash four heart tricks. A remedy is available. Do you remember it?

Of course you do! You must hold up the ♡A for two rounds, to remove East's hearts in case he has the ◇K. How does the play go?

You allow West's ♡K to win the first trick. He continues with the ♡Q and you allow that card to win too. You win the third round of hearts, discarding a club from dummy.

You now lead the ◇3 and play dummy's ◇Q. When the finesse wins, you return to your hand with the ♣K (or the ♠A, it makes no difference) and lead the ◇4, finessing the ◇J. The finesse wins and East follows suit. There is only one diamond still out. When you play dummy's ◇A, the ◇K falls from West. Dummy's last two diamonds are good and you will make an overtrick: two spades, one heart, five diamonds and two clubs. (If West had started with ◇K976, you would have returned to your hand again and finessed the ◇10, taking three finesses in the suit!)

When the cards lie as in the diagram, with West holding the ◇K, your hold-up play in hearts is not actually necessary. It was still the right play, because it would allow you to make the game when East held the ◇K.

> **PLAN: I will hold up the ♡A until the third round and then play a low diamond to dummy's ◇Q. If the finesse wins, I will return to my hand with the ♣K and finesse the ◇J. If this wins and diamonds break 3-2, I will play the ◇A, followed by the rest of the diamonds, and score ten tricks.**

PROBLEM 53

♠ K 8 5
♡ A J 6 3
◇ A K 10 2
♣ K 7

♠Q led

♠ A 6
♡ 10 8 2
◇ 8 4 3
♣ Q J 10 9 6

West	North	East	South
	1◇	pass	1NT
pass	2NT	pass	3NT
all pass			

West leads the ♠Q against 3NT. What is your plan for the contract?

Your first move is to count the top tricks. You have two in spades and one in hearts. In diamonds, the ace and king will give you two more top tricks. In clubs you start with none, although you are doubtless hoping to establish a few tricks. That gives you a total of just five:

Top Tricks: ♠ 2   ♡ 1   ◇ 2   ♣ 0   Total: 5

You need to find four extra tricks. The club suit will deliver the required number of tricks but you must make sure you will be able to score the tricks that you establish. How will you play the contract?

POINT TO REMEMBER _____

The hold-up is a valuable weapon for the defenders as well as for declarer. When you lead the ♣K on this deal, hoping to set up several club tricks, the defenders may well try to inconvenience you by holding up the ♣A for one round.

SOLUTION 53

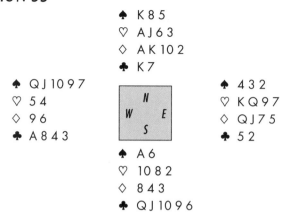

```
                    ♠ K 8 5
                    ♡ A J 6 3
                    ◇ A K 10 2
                    ♣ K 7
  ♠ Q J 10 9 7            N           ♠ 4 3 2
  ♡ 5 4          W             E      ♡ K Q 9 7
  ◇ 9 6                   S           ◇ Q J 7 5
  ♣ A 8 4 3                           ♣ 5 2
                    ♠ A 6
                    ♡ 10 8 2
                    ◇ 8 4 3
                    ♣ Q J 10 9 6
```

West leads the ♠Q against 3NT and you have these top tricks:

Top Tricks: ♠ 2　♡ 1　◇ 2　♣ 0　Total: 5

You can easily establish four more tricks from the club suit but you must make sure that you have an entry to the South hand to cash them. Everything depends on your play to the first trick. Will you win with the ♠A or the ♠K?

Let's see what will happen if you mistakenly win in your hand with the ♠A (using up an important entry prematurely). When you play the ♣6 to dummy's ♣K, the defenders will allow this to win. A second round of clubs goes to the ♣Q and West's ♣A. West continues spades and you have no entry to the good clubs in your hand! You will go at least one down.

At Trick 1 you must win with dummy's ♠K, preserving the ♠A entry to your hand. Now everything is easy. You lead the ♣K and West is welcome to hold up his ♣A. You continue clubs and West will have to take his ace at some stage. Whatever he returns, you will be able to cross to your ♠A to enjoy the established cards in the club suit. Nine tricks will be yours.

> **PLAN: I will win the first trick with the ♠K and lead the ♣K, continuing clubs until they take the ♣A. I can then win their return, cross to the ♠A and score the established club tricks.**

POINT TO REMEMBER

Many contracts depend on winning the opening lead in the right hand. You may have to plan the whole play before deciding where you should win the first trick.

PROBLEM 54

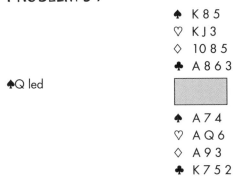

♠Q led

♠ K 8 5
♡ K J 3
◇ 10 8 5
♣ A 8 6 3

♠ A 7 4
♡ A Q 6
◇ A 9 3
♣ K 7 5 2

West	North	East	South
			1NT
pass	3NT	all pass	

West leads the ♠Q against 3NT. Before winning the first trick, you must make a plan. (Have we mentioned that before?) You count your top tricks, hoping that it will come to nine, and find this result:

Top Tricks: ♠ 2   ♡ 3   ◇ 1   ♣ 2   **Total: 8**

You have eight top tricks and will therefore need to create one extra trick from somewhere. You look at each suit in turn and ask yourself, 'Can I create an extra trick from this suit? How will the defenders' cards need to lie to allow me to create an extra trick?'

SOLUTION 54

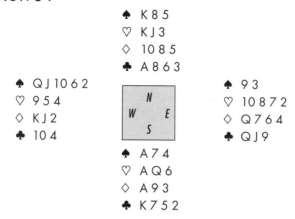

```
              ♠ K 8 5
              ♡ K J 3
              ◇ 10 8 5
              ♣ A 8 6 3
♠ Q J 10 6 2                      ♠ 9 3
♡ 9 5 4          N                ♡ 10 8 7 2
◇ K J 2      W       E            ◇ Q 7 6 4
♣ 10 4           S               ♣ Q J 9
              ♠ A 7 4
              ♡ A Q 6
              ◇ A 9 3
              ♣ K 7 5 2
```

West leads the ♠Q against 3NT and these are your top tricks:

Top Tricks: ♠ 2   ♡ 3   ◇ 1   ♣ 2   Total: 8

With eight top tricks, you will need one more to give you the game. When you look at the spades, hearts and diamonds, it is clear that none of those suits can give you an extra trick, no matter how the defenders' cards lie. The club suit does give you a chance. How will the defenders' cards have to break for you to be able to establish an extra trick from the clubs?

If the defenders' clubs break 3-2, you can establish one extra club trick. When you play the ♣A and ♣K, both defenders following, there will be just one club out. You will give up a club trick on the third round — playing a low club from each hand and allowing a defender to win the trick. Since the defenders will then have no clubs left, you can score an extra club trick. How does the play go?

You win the first trick in either hand. There are two good reasons why you should not hold up in spades. The first is that the defenders might switch to diamonds, where you have only one stopper. The second is that there is no purpose in a hold-up on this deal. Your plan is to give up a club trick and it will not help you at all to have held up in spades.

You play the ♣A and ♣K, winning the first two rounds of clubs. Next you lead a low club and allow East to win the trick with the ♣Q. When you regain the lead, you will score an extra trick with dummy's ♣8. This will bring your total to nine.

> **PLAN: I will win the spade lead and play the ♣A and ♣K. If clubs break 3-2, I will give up a club trick and score an extra trick in clubs.**

POINT TO REMEMBER

By giving up a trick in a suit, you may establish an extra winner.

PROBLEM 55

♠ A 9 6
♡ A 8 5
◇ 9 5 2
♣ Q 10 9 7

♡Q led

♠ K Q 4
♡ K 6 3 2
◇ A K 4
♣ J 3 2

West	North	East	South
			1NT
pass	3NT	all pass	

West leads the ♡Q against your contract of 3NT. How will you plan the play? You start with these top tricks:

Top Tricks: ♠ 3   ♡ 2   ◇ 2   ♣ 0   Total: 7

With seven top tricks, you will need two more tricks to make 3NT. Which suit gives you a chance to do this? How will you play the hand?

SOLUTION 55

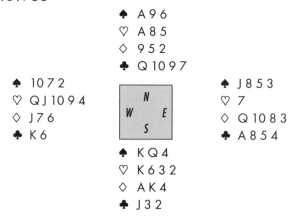

```
              ♠ A 9 6
              ♥ A 8 5
              ◇ 9 5 2
              ♣ Q 10 9 7
♠ 10 7 2                          ♠ J 8 5 3
♥ Q J 10 9 4      N               ♥ 7
◇ J 7 6       W       E           ◇ Q 10 8 3
♣ K 6             S               ♣ A 8 5 4
              ♠ K Q 4
              ♥ K 6 3 2
              ◇ A K 4
              ♣ J 3 2
```

West leads the ♥Q against your 3NT contract and you have seven top tricks:

Top Tricks: ♠ 3   ♥ 2   ◇ 2   ♣ 0   Total: 7

There is no chance of creating extra tricks in spades or diamonds. In hearts you could create one extra trick if hearts broke 3-3. Such a break is very unlikely after West has decided to lead the suit. Anyway, you need to develop *two* more tricks, not one. In clubs the situation is brighter. You can create two extra tricks by knocking out the ace and the king. How does the play go?

You win the first trick with the ♥K and lead the ♣J, playing the high card from the shorter side first. Let's say that East wins the trick with the ♣A. He has no heart to return, so he switches to the ◇3. You rise with the ◇A and lead a low club, West winning with the king. Whatever he returns, you will now cash nine top tricks, including the two extra tricks that you have established in clubs.

> **PLAN: I will win with the ♥K and lead the ♣J, knocking out one of the defenders' club stoppers. When I regain the lead I will continue to play clubs, knocking out the other stopper.**

POINT TO REMEMBER

Establishing a suit at notrump often involves giving the defenders a trick or two in the suit, so you can make the remaining tricks there. Sometimes this is a question of playing an honor to knock out the defenders' stoppers. Sometimes you will duck a round or two instead, waiting for your remaining cards to become high.

PROBLEM 56

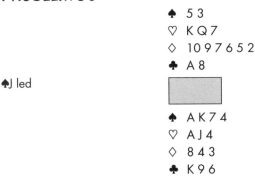

♠ 5 3
♡ K Q 7
◇ 1 0 9 7 6 5 2
♣ A 8

♠J led

♠ A K 7 4
♡ A J 4
◇ 8 4 3
♣ K 9 6

West	North	East	South
			1NT
pass	3NT	all pass	

North has only 9 points, not normally quite enough to raise a 15-17 point 1NT to 3NT. He decides that his six-card diamond suit entitles him to add an extra point. Maybe partner will hold something useful in diamonds and will be able to establish the suit. How would you plan this contract when West leads the ♠J?

You count your top tricks and find this position:

Top Tricks: ♠ 2   ♡ 3   ◇ 0   ♣ 2   Total: 7

You need two extra tricks to make the game. There is no real prospect of making even one extra trick from spades, hearts or clubs. You will therefore need to establish the diamonds, despite the defenders holding the ace, king, queen and jack. How will the defenders' cards have to lie for this to be possible? How will you play the contract?

SOLUTION 56

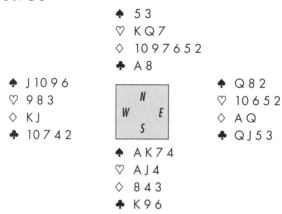

```
                  ♠  5 3
                  ♡  K Q 7
                  ◇  10 9 7 6 5 2
                  ♣  A 8
♠  J 10 9 6                        ♠  Q 8 2
♡  9 8 3          N                ♡  10 6 5 2
◇  K J         W     E             ◇  A Q
♣  10 7 4 2       S                ♣  Q J 5 3
                  ♠  A K 7 4
                  ♡  A J 4
                  ◇  8 4 3
                  ♣  K 9 6
```

West leads the ♠J against 3NT and you have these top tricks:

Top Tricks: ♠ 2   ♡ 3   ◇ 0   ♣ 2   Total: 7

The only suit that offers any prospect of creating extra tricks is diamonds. Even though you are missing the four top honors in the suit, you will have time to establish it when the defenders' diamonds break 2-2. How will the play go?

You win the spade lead with the ♠K and lead the ◇3, West playing the ◇J. East overtakes with the ◇Q and returns the ♠Q. You win with the ♠A and play another diamond. West plays the ◇K and East overtakes with the ◇A! The defenders have no more cards left in diamonds, so you have established four extra winners. The defenders score two spade tricks, to go with their two diamond tricks. The remaining tricks are yours and you make the 3NT contract.

> **PLAN: I will win the first trick and play a diamond. I will win the spade return and play another diamond. When the defenders' diamonds split 2-2, the diamond suit will be established. Unless the defenders can then cash three spade tricks, I will make the game.**

POINT TO REMEMBER

Even when the defenders hold several high cards in your long suit, it may be possible to establish the suit. When the defenders' cards break evenly, their honors will fall together on the early tricks.

PROBLEM 57

♠ 8 7 4
♡ A 8 2
♢ K J 10 9 4
♣ Q 7

♠Q led

♠ A K
♡ K 10 6 5
♢ 6 5 2
♣ A J 6 3

West	North	East	South
			1NT
pass	3NT	all pass	

West leads the ♠Q against 3NT. How will you plan the play?

Combining your hand with the dummy, you start with these top tricks:

Top Tricks: ♠ 2 ♡ 2 ♢ 0 ♣ 1 Total: 5

With only five top tricks, you need an extra four tricks to make the game. The defenders have already knocked out one of your spade stoppers and will surely persist with that suit when they win the lead. What chance do you have of scoring four extra tricks before they can make enough tricks to defeat you?

POINT TO REMEMBER

When you need a piece of good luck to make a contract, look on the bright side and assume that you will be lucky. Bridge is not a game for pessimists!

SOLUTION 57

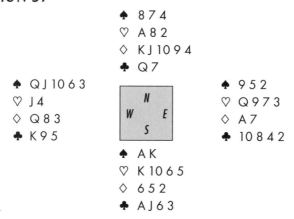

```
              ♠ 8 7 4
              ♡ A 8 2
              ◇ K J 10 9 4
              ♣ Q 7
♠ Q J 10 6 3                    ♠ 9 5 2
♡ J 4          N                ♡ Q 9 7 3
◇ Q 8 3     W     E             ◇ A 7
♣ K 9 5          S              ♣ 10 8 4 2
              ♠ A K
              ♡ K 10 6 5
              ◇ 6 5 2
              ♣ A J 6 3
```

West leads the ♠Q against 3NT and you have these top tricks:

Top Tricks: ♠ 2 ♡ 2 ◇ 0 ♣ 1 Total: 5

How can you make four extra tricks? You might make one extra trick from the heart suit or from the club suit. Since you need four extra tricks and you have only one spade stopper remaining, you must try to make all four extra tricks from the diamond suit. How will the defenders' diamonds have to lie for this to be possible?

You will need West to hold the ◇Q. If that is the case, you can finesse two or three times against the queen and create four extra diamond tricks. How does the play go?

You win the spade lead and lead the ◇2 to dummy's ◇J. You are in luck! Since East does not hold the ◇Q he has only two options — he can win with the ◇A or play the ◇7, allowing dummy's ◇J to win. It makes no difference what he does. Let's say that he wins with the ◇A and returns a spade, removing your last stopper in the suit.

You then lead the ◇5, playing dummy's ◇10. (You are repeating your previous finesse against the ◇Q.) When East follows with the ◇7, there is only one diamond still out. You play the ◇K and the ◇Q falls from West. Dummy's last two diamonds are good and your four extra diamond tricks will give you the contract.

> **PLAN: I will win the spade lead and finesse the ◇J. If East wins with the ◇A, I will repeat the diamond finesse and score four diamond tricks for the contract. If instead the ◇J wins, I will return to my hand with the ♡K and finesse the ◇10.**

POINT TO REMEMBER

When you are trying to establish a long suit, you can often take a finesse to assist the process.

PROBLEM 58

♠ 7 5
♡ A J 7
◇ 9 5 4 2
♣ A J 7 2

♠4 led

♠ A K
♡ K Q 5
◇ J 10 8 7
♣ Q 6 5 3

West	North	East	South
			1NT
pass	3NT	all pass	

West leads the ♠4 against 3NT, East playing the ♠Q. How will you play the contract?

You have two top tricks in the spade suit and three more in hearts. You have no top tricks in diamonds and one in clubs. This is the summary:

Top Tricks: ♠ 2   ♡ 3   ◇ 0   ♣ 1   Total: 6

With only one spade stopper remaining, you need three extra tricks in a hurry. You must look for a way to create four tricks from the club suit. This will then give you the three extra tricks that you need.

Think carefully about how the defenders' clubs must lie to allow you to score all four club tricks. How will you play the contract? In particular, how will you play the club suit?

SOLUTION 58

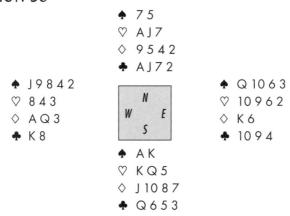

```
                ♠ 7 5
                ♡ A J 7
                ◇ 9 5 4 2
                ♣ A J 7 2
♠ J 9 8 4 2                      ♠ Q 10 6 3
♡ 8 4 3          N              ♡ 10 9 6 2
◇ A Q 3       W     E           ◇ K 6
♣ K 8            S              ♣ 10 9 4
                ♠ A K
                ♡ K Q 5
                ◇ J 10 8 7
                ♣ Q 6 5 3
```

West leads the ♠4 against 3NT, East playing the ♠Q. This is the top trick position:

Top Tricks: ♠ 2   ♡ 3   ◇ 0   ♣ 1   Total: 6

You need another three tricks to make 3NT and these must come from the club suit. How will the defenders' clubs have to lie to allow you to score four club tricks?

You can make all four club tricks in just one situation, when West holds two clubs including the king. How will you play the suit to take advantage of this situation?

After winning the spade lead, you must lead the ♣3 (not the ♣Q) from the South hand. West plays the ♣8 and you finesse dummy's ♣J. This wins the trick. Since you can make the contract only when West started with a doubleton ♣K, you next play the ♣A. Hallelujah, the king drops! A low club to the ♣Q draws East's last club and you score a fourth club trick with a very small card. The game is yours.

Think back to the chapter on finesses, where we mentioned that you should lead an honor in a finesse position only when you held two neighboring honors between the hands. Here you should not lead the ♣Q because you hold only one neighboring honor (the ♣J). Do you see what will happen if you mistakenly lead the ♣Q? West will cover with the ♣K and dummy's ♣A will win the trick. Dummy's ♣J wins the second round of clubs but East's ♣10 is then the top club. You could make two extra club tricks, by giving up a round of clubs. This would bring your total to just eight and you would go one down.

> **PLAN: I will win the spade lead and play a low club to the ♣J. If West began with two clubs including the king, the ♣A will drop his ♣K. When that happens, I will make the three extra club tricks that I need.**

PROBLEM 59

♠ 8 3
♡ 9 8 4
◇ J 9 5
♣ A 8 6 5 2

♠Q led

```
┌─────────┐
│         │
└─────────┘
```

♠ A K 4
♡ A K 7 5
◇ A 10 6
♣ K 7 3

West	North	East	South
			2NT
pass	3NT	all pass	

West leads the ♠Q against 3NT. How will you play the contract?

When you count your top tricks, you find this position:

Top Tricks: ♠ 2 ♡ 2 ◇ 1 ♣ 2 Total: 7

You have seven top tricks and will need two more to bring a smile to partner's lips. It looks like you will have to establish the club suit. How do you plan to play the club suit so that you can enjoy two extra club tricks?

POINT TO REMEMBER

When dummy is very weak, you have to pay particular attention to your entries. If your plan is to set up a long suit in dummy, will you be able to reach the established cards?

SOLUTION 59

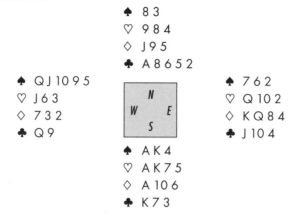

```
                    ♠ 8 3
                    ♡ 9 8 4
                    ◇ J 9 5
                    ♣ A 8 6 5 2
♠ Q J 10 9 5                        ♠ 7 6 2
♡ J 6 3          N                  ♡ Q 10 2
◇ 7 3 2      W        E             ◇ K Q 8 4
♣ Q 9            S                  ♣ J 10 4
                    ♠ A K 4
                    ♡ A K 7 5
                    ◇ A 10 6
                    ♣ K 7 3
```

West leads the ♠Q against your 3NT. You start with seven top tricks:

Top Tricks: ♠ 2   ♡ 2   ◇ 1   ♣ 2   Total: 7

You need two extra tricks and it is natural to seek these from clubs, your longest suit. If the defenders' clubs break 3-2, you can establish the suit. The fourth and fifth rounds of clubs will then deliver two extra tricks. However, you will need an entry to dummy to reach the extra tricks in clubs. How can you arrange this?

You win the spade lead since there is no reason to hold up. Suppose your next move is to play the king and ace on the first two rounds of clubs. You would then have to give up a round of clubs to the defenders. The club suit would break 3-2, yes, and dummy's ♣8 and ♣6 would then be good. They would not bring you any 'extra tricks', however, since there would be no entry to reach them!

Instead you should lead the ♣K on the first round of clubs (a high card from the shorter side) and then duck a round of clubs — play low cards from both hands. You lead the ♣3 and play the ♣5 from dummy. West will win the trick with the ♣Q. You win the spade return in your hand and can now enjoy the benefit of ducking an early round of clubs — you cross to dummy by leading the ♣7 to the ace. You score the extra tricks that you need with the ♣8 and ♣6. You have made four club tricks and two spade tricks. The ♡AK and ◇A will bring your total to nine.

> **PLAN: I will win the spade lead and play the ♣K. I will then duck the second round of clubs. After winning the spade return, I will cross to the ♣A to score two more club tricks (if the suit breaks 3-2). I will then have nine top tricks.**

POINT TO REMEMBER

By ducking an early round of dummy's long suit, you can preserve dummy's high card as an entry.

PROBLEM 60 (a little more difficult)

```
            ♠ A Q 7
            ♡ J 7 3
            ♢ J 10 9 8 5
            ♣ J 2
♠J led
            ┌──────────┐
            │          │
            └──────────┘
            ♠ K 5 4
            ♡ A 9 6 2
            ♢ A K
            ♣ A 9 5 3
```

West	North	East	South
			1♣
pass	1♢	pass	2NT
pass	3NT	all pass	

With 18 high-card points you are too strong to open 1NT. You open 1♣ and jump to 2NT on the next round. North has enough to raise to 3NT and West leads the ♠J. You will not want to go down on the very last problem in the book, so the time has come to make a plan! How many top tricks do you have?

Top Tricks: ♠ 3   ♡ 1   ♢ 2   ♣ 1   Total: 7

You need two extra tricks and the prospects are unattractive in spades, hearts and clubs. You must turn your attention to the diamond suit. How can you establish the diamonds and score the two extra tricks that you need?

POINT TO REMEMBER

By giving up one trick in a suit, you can often establish extra tricks there.

SOLUTION 60

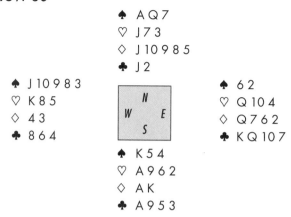

```
            ♠ A Q 7
            ♡ J 7 3
            ◇ J 10 9 8 5
            ♣ J 2
♠ J 10 9 8 3              ♠ 6 2
♡ K 8 5          N        ♡ Q 10 4
◇ 4 3        W     E      ◇ Q 7 6 2
♣ 8 6 4          S        ♣ K Q 10 7
            ♠ K 5 4
            ♡ A 9 6 2
            ◇ A K
            ♣ A 9 5 3
```

West leads the ♠J against your 3NT and you start with these top tricks:

Top Tricks: ♠ 3   ♡ 1   ◇ 2   ♣ 1   Total: 7

The two extra tricks that you need will have to come from the diamond suit. How can you plan the play so that you will be able to knock out the defenders' ◇Q and return to dummy to enjoy the established extra tricks?

The key moment comes on the very first trick. Since you have plenty of entries to the South hand and there are relatively few entries to dummy, you should win the spade lead with the ♠K. This will leave the ♠A and ♠Q as entries to the dummy later.

The next move is to play the ◇A and ◇K, the high cards from the shorter side. You then cross to dummy with the ♠Q and lead the ◇J. East wins with the ◇Q and you throw a club (or a heart) from your hand. You win East's return, whichever suit he plays, and return to dummy with the ♠A. You can then score two extra diamond tricks with the ◇10 and ◇9. Your eventual total of nine tricks will consist of three spades, one heart, four diamonds and one club.

> **PLAN: I will win with the ♠K and play the ◇A and ◇K. I will then cross to dummy with the ♠Q and lead the ◇J, giving up a trick to the ◇Q. I will win the return, cross to the ♠A and score two extra tricks in diamonds.**

POINT TO REMEMBER _____

When you can win the opening lead in either hand, think carefully which hand will be better. You will often need to win in the hand containing more honor cards (entries). By doing so, you conserve the entries to the weaker hand.

GLOSSARY OF BRIDGE TERMS

B

Block Situation where the position of one or more high cards prevents the easy playing of a suit. For example, AK opposite QJ86.

Break If the defenders' clubs 'break 3-2', one of them holds 3 clubs and the other holds 2. You might say 'I needed a 3-2 club break to make the contract.'

C

Cash When you lead a card that is a winner, you can be said to 'cash the card'. You are converting it into a trick, similar to when you cash a check into real money.

Clear a suit You clear a suit by leading it until an opponent wins with his side's last stopper in the suit. Your remaining cards in that suit are then good.

Continue Lead a suit that has previously been played. 'West led the ◇A and continued with the ◇K.'

Cover When a high card is led from one hand, the next player may cover with a higher card. 'Declarer led the ♠Q and West covered with the ♠K.'

Cross To move to the opposite hand by leading to a high card there. 'Declarer crossed to dummy with the ◇A.'

D

Danger hand (or dangerous defender)
A defender who can cause you some damage if he wins a trick. For example, he may have some winners to cash, enough to beat your contract.

Discard
Noun or verb to describe the action of playing a card in a different suit (not a trump) when you cannot follow suit, as in 'Declarer discarded a diamond loser on the ♣A.'

Double finesse
If you take two finesses in the same suit, this is called a double finesse. For example, with ♣AJ10 in dummy opposite your ♣762 you would finesse the ♣10 first. If this lost, you would finesse the ♣J next. Similarly with ◊AQ10.

E

Entry
A high card that will allow you to reach a particular hand. For example: 'The queen of trumps was my only entry to the dummy.'

Establish a suit Play a suit until all the remaining cards are winners.

F

Finesse
An attempt to make a trick with a card that is not a top winner, usually by leading towards it. For example with ♣A76 opposite ♣KJ4, you can play the ♣A and then lead the ♣6 to the ♣J, hoping that the ♣Q lies in front of the ♣J.

G

Give up a trick
To allow the defenders to win a trick. For example, the purpose may be to establish the remainder of the suit.

Good cards
Cards that have been established and will each be worth a trick. 'Declarer crossed to dummy's ◊A to reach the two good hearts.'

H

Holding
The cards that you hold in a suit. 'My club holding was king-queen doubleton.'

Honor
One of the top five cards in a suit: ace, king, queen, jack or ten.

K

Knock out
To remove a defender's stopper in a suit. 'I can establish three extra tricks by knocking out the ♣A.'

L

Lead a card When you play the first card to a new trick, you are said to lead the card. For example: 'Declarer led the ♣Q from dummy.'

Lead towards a card You lead a low card from one hand towards a high card (such as a king) in the other hand, hoping that a higher card (such as the ace) lies with the defender playing second to the trick.

Line of play An intended sequence of playing the cards. 'My intended line of play was to draw trumps and establish the club suit.'

Long-trump hand The hand (dummy or declarer's hand) that contains more trumps than the hand opposite.

Losers Cards in your hand that may not win a trick. For example, ♡AK7 contains one loser because the ♡7 may not win a trick.

M

Master A card that has become the highest card left in a suit because the other higher cards have been played.

O

Overruff Noun or verb describing the action of ruffing with a higher trump than the one just used by an opponent. 'Declarer ruffed with the ♠6 and West overruffed with the ♠8.'

Overtake To play a higher card than one that has already been played by your side. 'Declarer led the ♡J and overtook with dummy's ♡Q.'

P

Play a card On each trick all four players play a card. For example: 'West led the ◊A and East played the ◊8.' The phrase has a different meaning from 'lead a card', which refers to the first card played in a trick.

Q

Quick losers Tricks that the defenders will be able to score as soon as they win the lead.

R

Repeat finesse   To finesse against a defender's honor for the second time. For example, you lead low towards the ♠AQJ and finesse the jack, winning the trick. Later you would repeat the finesse, playing low to the queen.

Return   If you are in dummy, you can 'return to your hand' by leading to a top card there. If the defender in the East seat wins with the ◊A, he can 'return another diamond.' In other words, he leads another diamond on the next trick.

Rise with a card   To play a high card in the second seat. 'Declarer led towards dummy's ♠Q and West rose with the ♠K.'

Round   A complete trick in a suit. 'Declarer drew two rounds of trumps.'

Ruff   Noun or verb to describe the action of trumping a card, as in 'Declarer took a club ruff', or 'Declarer ruffed a diamond.'

Ruff high   Ruff with a master trump, to ensure a defender cannot overruff.

Run a suit   To play all the cards in a suit, scoring a trick with each card.

S

Safe hand (or safe defender)   A defender who cannot cause you any damage if he wins a trick. For example, he may have no cards left in the suit that was led against 3NT.

Sequence   Three or more honors that are consecutive, or nearly so. For example, the KQJ or KQ10.

Set up a suit   Play a suit until all the remaining cards are winners (an alternative term for 'establish a suit').

Short-trump hand   The hand (dummy or declarer's hand) that contains fewer trumps than the hand opposite.

Show out   Fail to follow suit. 'When I played the ◊A, West showed out.'

Side suit   One of the three suits that are not trumps. 'I had five top winners in the side suits.'

Slow losers   Tricks that the defenders will be able to score, once they have removed your stoppers in the suit.

Spot card   All cards from the nine down to the two are known as spot cards. The cards above the nine in rank are known as honor cards.

Stopper   A high card that prevents the opponents from scoring tricks in a suit.

Switch   Noun or verb describing the action of leading a different suit after winning a trick. 'East won with the ♣A and switched to the ♠J.'

T

Tenace   Two cards, usually honors, that are not adjacent. 'West had to lead into my ace-queen tenace.'

Throw   An alternative term for discard. 'I played dummy's ♡A and threw my club loser.'

Top Tricks   The tricks that declarer could cash immediately, if he so wished, both in his own hand and the dummy

W

Winner   A card that will win a trick if played. 'West played the ◇A and dummy's ◇K was then a winner.'

Master Point Press on the Internet

www.masterpointpress.com

Our main site, with information about our books and software, reviews and more.

www.teachbridge.com

Our site for bridge teachers and students — free downloadable support material for our books, helpful articles and more.

www.bridgeblogging.com

Read and comment on regular articles from MPP authors and other bridge notables.

www.ebooksbridge.com

Purchase downloadable electronic versions of MPP books and software.